ST ARTING A NURSERY

A PRACTICAL GUIDE FOR
ARLY-YEARS PROFESSIONALS

MARTIN PACE

NURSERY WORLD

A NURSERY WORLD BOOK

NURSERY WORLD

A NURSERY WORLD BOOK

First edition published in Great Britain by
TSL Education Ltd
Admiral House, 66-68 East Smithfield
London E1W 1BX

2 4 6 8 10 9 7 5 3 1

Copyright © 1999 TSL Education Limited, London

A CIP catalogue record for this book is available from the British Library

ISBN 1-84122-017-5

Printed and bound in Belgium

Editor: Ruth Thomson
Senior Art Editor: Nicola Liddiard
Commissioning Editor: Patricia Grogan
Illustration: Charlotte Combe

CONTENTS

INTRODUCTION

Starting a Nursery is designed to help you start your own successful nursery business and is written in 12 chapters, any of which can be accessed on its own or as part of the whole. If you are an early years professional and are keen to make the step from employee to employer, or if you have had some contact with the nursery sector and can see that nurseries are a rewarding business to become involved in, then this book will show you how to start. A few salutary words of warning, however, before you begin.

Before you make the shift from employee to employer, you will need to ask yourself if it is the right move for you. Not everyone is suited to running a business. If you make the decision to start, the biggest factor determining the success of the business will be you, so are you sure you want to do it?

If you are sure, then you will need to know your strengths and weaknesses. In order to evaluate your own potential and to decide if you are the right person with the necessary skills, ask yourself a few questions. For example, can you work long hours? Are you persistent enough under pressure to always keep going? Can you live with financial insecurity? Do you view failure as a learning opportunity? Do you recognise when you need help? Can you prioritise? Can you delegate? Is your health good?[1] If you decide to proceed, then this book, and others sources of information, will help you move forward.

If you have a family, you will want to involve them at the earliest stage. Starting and running your own business is a way of life rather than just a job and you will need considerable support, particularly during the early stages when you may suffer a number of setbacks. It is a fact that most people who start a business earn far less in the first few years than they expected, usually because the business income simply cannot support a substantial salary. So, you will need to be aware that this venture may affect detrimentally your standard of living, at least in the short term.

Before starting your venture, you will also need to analyse your motives to ensure that profit is not your sole aim, because if it is, it could cause your nursery business to fail. In the words of Rosemary Murphy, chief executive of the National Day Nurseries Association: 'You have massive responsibilities as an employer. Prospective owners have got to want to be in business. You can't do it just because you love children. There's no room in the market for people just doing it for pin money. Nor should you think of entering the market if you're only interested in money. Quality has got to be a priority.'[2]

As obvious as it may seem, providing a high standard of care for children is essential if

---

[1] There is a good self-assessment questionnaire in *Lloyds Bank Small Business Guide* by Sara Williams, Penguin (1987). Another source of self-questioning material can be found in *What Colour Is Your Parachute?* by Richard Bolles, Ten Speed Press (1970)
[2] *Starting a Nursery, Nursery World* (Summer 1999) p5

you are to succeed and you will need to pitch considerable resources at staff, training, equipment and management to ensure that quality is consistently top of your agenda. We have a moral and social responsibility to deliver the best in childcare but from a pragmatic perspective if you skimp on quality you run the risk of failing – as everyone in childcare knows, reputation is all.

The 12 chapters in the book take you through each step of the process of setting up a nursery, from market research and raising money to inspection legislation, staff recruitment and finding premises – one of the more difficult aspects of starting your own nursery.

So that you know others have had to negotiate the same difficulties as you, the last chapter provides case studies, designed to inspire the confidence you will need to see the process through.

If you are new to childcare and you are using this book as a starting point to understand the sector, then more research will be required to grasp fully the business of running a nursery and within each chapter there are pointers to other useful sources.

This book is not intended to influence your views or provide information regarding educational styles for children or different curricula[3]. Neither does it cover the specifics of setting up a company, which is information you can obtain from your bank manager or accountant. There are also many publications which cover company set-up[4].

The bibliography and useful addresses listed at the back of the book will help you seek out the additional information you need to start up a successful nursery business. Included are national childcare organisations and government departments but you will need to seek out local contacts, particularly when it comes to raising funds for your business.

There is currently a trend towards the construction of larger nurseries, and purpose-built facilities of 100+ places are becoming increasingly common. Throughout the book it is generally assumed that a medium-sized nursery is one of 45-60 places and that a large nursery is 65+ places.

Finally, if a nursery is to be profitable then the childcare needs to be of the highest standard. The key to delivering quality childcare is to value staff; a view which is repeated throughout this book.

This book is dedicated to Jo and Jessica.

[3] Before opening your own nursery you should read *Children First* by Penelope Leach, Penguin (1994)
[4] S. Williams *Lloyds Bank Small Business Guide* Penguin (1987)

1: THE NURSERY MARKETPLACE

ALTHOUGH THE NUMBER OF UNDER-FIVES is forecast to decline slightly over the next few years, the childcare sector represents a potentially buoyant marketplace for the foreseeable future, offering greater opportunity than ever before for would-be nursery owners.

DEMAND

The predicted decline in the number of under-fives belies the true picture of rising demand for childcare in the UK. At present, demand outstrips supply and the number of working women with children is increasing. Indications are that this trend is likely to continue.

More than half the women in the UK are in some form of employment[1] and it is women with pre-school children that are the growing proportion of the workforce. More women are now having their children when they have progressed further in their careers and have achieved higher financial status. The trend has led to increased demand for childcare, as this group of women often seeks to maintain its status by returning to the workplace as soon as possible

[1] *Social Trends 28* Office for National Statistics

after childbirth and are generally more able to afford childcare fees.

Another factor influencing the growth of demand for childcare is the movement of young professionals away from the extended family. This group of people tends to move into new towns where employment opportunities are high and there is an adequate supply of family housing, and the attendant mortgages often require both parents to work.

Companies which have invested heavily in training professional and managerial staff depend on the levels of experience of their staff and can ill afford to lose them when they decide to have a family. Many responsible employers now see childcare as the keystone of their 'family friendly' benefits package aimed at retaining staff.

Rising skills shortages combined with falling numbers of school leavers over the next decade will result in more women being encouraged to remain in the workforce after childbirth. The industries that tend to provide childcare for their employees are those already struggling to recruit and retain skilled staff, principally financial institutions, hospitals, universities and pharmaceutical companies.

In addition, recent Governments have recognised that childcare is essential to allow parents to work, but it is the current Labour Government that is investing more in childcare than any previous administration.

Its National Childcare Strategy aims to provide good quality and affordable childcare for children aged nought to 14. Under its Early Years Development and Childcare Plans, local authorities are expected to develop childcare provision by involving statutory, private and voluntary providers. There is now funding for part-time education for all four-year-olds and £390m set aside to provide 190,000 free places for three-year-olds up to 2002. The Lottery New Opportunities Fund will allocate £170 million in England to help fund out-of-school childcare. And Labour's Childcare Tax Credit, which forms part

of the Working Families Tax Credit, will cover up to 70 per cent of low- and middle-income families' childcare costs, where the family pays up to £100 a week in childcare for one child and up to £150 a week for two children or more. The income ceilings are around £22,000 a year for families with one child in childcare and around £30,000 for families with more than one child in childcare.

As long as work opportunities exist for women in the economy, and the demographics indicate that this is set to continue, it is reasonable to expect that demand for childcare, assisted by Government initiatives, will continue to rise for the next five to ten years.

CHILDCARE CHOICES

Where parents need childcare, and there is no extended family to provide that care, the choices of provision for the under-fives are limited to:

- *nannies, who usually look after children in the parent's home*

- *childminders, who usually look after children in the childminder's own home and are registered by the local authority*

- *playgroups, which operate morning or afternoon sessions for children aged three to five, and often involve parents in providing part of the care*

- *Local Authority (LA) Day Nurseries, which offer full day care*

- *LA nursery schools, which offer care for three- to four-year-olds for mornings or afternoons only*

- *Infant classes attached to Local Education Authority (LEA) schools, which offer care to rising fours (at present) for a school day*

- *Workplace nurseries, which operate as private day nurseries for children of employees of a particular company*

- *Private day nurseries, which offer full day care (often from 8.00am to 6.00pm or beyond) to children aged three months to five years*

Playgroups, LA nursery schools and LEA infant classes still cater for the majority of children but only provide part-time care. LA day nurseries are fast disappearing, with the number of places falling by about one third between 1986 and 1996[2]. The rising demand is being met primarily by private day nurseries.

DAY NURSERY PROVISION

Historically, private day nursery care in the UK has been

[2] Market research carried out by Greenhouse Childcare Consultancy

provided by single owner-operators in converted residential properties, providing around 40 or 50 places. In recent years the sector has changed and there has been an increase in the amount of day nurseries and in the types of provision. Until more recently, most places were for the over-twos. It is only in the last ten years that baby places have been provided in any significant numbers.

The number of independent day nurseries rose from 1,413 in 1987 to nearly 5,500 by 1997, an increase of 381 per cent[3]. Over the same period nursery places rose by 457 per cent to around 172,000[4]. Clearly, provision is increasing dramatically and the rate of increase surpasses most other sectors in the UK. However, there are still not enough nursery places to meet demand and many nurseries have waiting lists, particularly for baby places. Research figures from 1995 showed that there were 3.2 million under-fives in England and only 1.6 million childcare places across all types of provision[5].

Many of the recently built, larger nurseries have been developed and operated by nursery 'chains' – nursery operators

[3] *Independent Day Nursery Workforce Survey* prepared by The Local Government Management Board (October 1998)

[4] ibid

[5] Market research carried out by Greenhouse Childcare Consultancy

offering childcare in multiple locations. Parallels have been drawn with the growth witnessed in the elderly care sector over the last 20 years and, significantly, some of the new growth in childcare provision is funded by operators in the elderly care sector.

In addition, the last decade has seen an increasing number of employers develop 'workplace' nurseries, which involve the employer providing the capital for a childcare facility on or near the place of work. There are still many workplace nurseries under development as employers reap the benefit of improved staff retention. However, more recently there is a trend for nursery operators to risk their own capital to provide a nursery nearby an employer and enter an agreement with the employer to reserve places. This arrangement benefits both nursery owner and employer. The nursery owner has greater control over the type of childcare provided while the employer receives a more flexible service with little, or no, capital outlay.

The volume of day nursery provision varies geographically and demand can be much higher in some locations than others. Swindon which had only four private day nurseries in 1990 now has nearly 20. Growth has come from demand from employers competing for staff and the almost constant development of new housing. A new town attracts young families without the benefit of their extended family to look after the children.

In general, the private day nursery sector is still in an early stage of development but is ripe for considerable growth. A market research survey found that of the 20 nursery operators canvassed, all reported that their business had suffered virtually no damage during the last recession and that they have little fear of the next potential downturn in the economy[6].

Many of the larger players plan to grow quickly and achieve greater market share but there is a significant window of opportunity for smaller operators to get into a profitable growth market. There are not many large chains at present but the private day nursery chains and company-sponsored childcare providers in the table opposite are in the commanding position:

[6] Market research carried out by Greenhouse Childcare Consultancy

CHILDCARE PROVIDER	Number of nurseries November 1999*
Asquith Court	60
The Birrell Collection	5
Bright Horizons	7
Bringing up Baby	7
Busy Bees	23
Careshare	9
Child & Co	11
Child Base	17
Childcare Enterprise	13
Childcare Partners/Buffer Bear	11
Copperbeech	13
Early Years	10
Happy Child	10
Jigsaw Group	25
Just Learning	15
Kids Unlimited	32
KinderCare	2
Kinderquest	38
Leapfrog Day Nurseries	12
Nurseryworks	8
Petits Enfants	8
Princess Christian/Nord Anglia	27
Saplings	3
Teddies	16
* Source: *Nursery Chains, Nursery World* (November 1999)	

That there is a need for more nurseries is apparent. As shown by the demographics, demand will continue to rise, assisted by Government initiatives and caring employers. However, a new childcare venture in the current climate is not without risks and staff shortages are perhaps the greatest threat to the quality of childcare at present (see Chapter 11: Management and staffing).

Of significant concern to operators is the loss of a proportion of numbers of four-year-olds to schools and the same could happen to three-year-olds as the number of Government-funded places for this age group rises. Losing three-year-olds to schools would leave private nurseries caring for ever younger children, who require higher ratios of carer to child, and the increased staff costs are likely to result in lower profitability.

In addition, there is a rising number of well-funded new chains in the sector, all planning rapid growth, and these key players will be seeking to lock out some of the smaller operators in many areas. If the childcare sector progresses in a similar way to that of elderly care, then a number of takeovers and amalgamations will give rise to a handful of 'giants', with significant market share. At present the market share of all the major chains (including those not listed above) is no greater than 10 per cent. Perhaps in a few years we will see five or six companies controlling up to one quarter of the market.

It is appropriate to draw the conclusion that the next few years will see many new entrants, small and large, into the childcare sector. And, if you bear in mind that any nursery draws 80 per cent of its business from a five-mile radius of its location, what becomes clear is the fact that that there will always be room for the single owner/operator, providing quality childcare to a local market.

2: MARKET RESEARCH

WOULD-BE NURSERY OWNERS tend to ignore market research, often because they do not know where to start. However, if you are to attract funding to set up your business, you will need to show that you have conducted market research, and this chapter should enable you to prepare a full appraisal of your nursery in relation to its marketplace.

THE NEED FOR MARKET RESEARCH

Market research is not rocket science. It is simply a set of logical steps that will establish that the area you have chosen for your nursery:

- *has enough children to support your nursery*

- *will enable you to charge a high enough fee*

- *will enable you to fill your nursery quickly enough and stay full, so that you can make a modest profit (you won't be able to make an 'immodest' profit unless you are charging an unusually high fee or you are paying very low wages)*

Without market research your project will be in the lap of the gods. Of course you may still succeed, but through luck rather than good management. There is no doubt that a 'gut feeling' about a location or area is one of the most reliable indicators but market research will help translate that feeling into something more communicable. The research process will also help define the service that you should offer and ensure that it responds to local needs. Decisions about the age of children, hours of service, whether to provide lunches included in the price, the curriculum you adopt and so on will all be refined by your research.

So where do you start? The first thing to do is to establish that the location you have selected is a good one in relation to your customers, or 'marketplace'.

THE MARKETPLACE

Most nurseries tend to draw 80 per cent of their customers from a radius of five miles from their location; this area can be defined as the marketplace. (The exception to this rule is the 'workplace' nursery where childcare is provided for children of employees in a particular organisation. The marketplace is then the distance that the employer draws on, which can often be greater than five miles.)

For ease of measurement and for effective marketing, this marketplace can be divided into three segments: the 'residential', the 'corporate' and the 'commuting'.

Residential market

The residential market comprises people who live in a five-mile radius of the nursery. You will need to analyse this market to establish that:

• *there are enough children of pre-school age in the area to sustain a nursery (or another nursery if you are not the first in the area)*

• *parents can afford your anticipated fee*

• *there is a need for childcare (perhaps there is a large number of families where both parents work)*

• *parents are likely to choose nursery care over the alternatives, such as a relative, childminder or nanny*

• *the status quo will not alter dramatically to your detriment (for example, residents are leaving, or likely to leave, the area)*

Corporate market

The corporate market covers people who work within a three-mile radius of the nursery. In this instance, you will want to establish:

• *how many people are working in the area*

• *what percentage of them are likely to want to use your nursery*

• *how much they will be able to afford to pay and whether the company is likely to subsidise the childcare*

• *employment trends in the area (for example, are new companies moving into the area or are the existing ones moving out?)*

Commuting market

The commuting market is made up of people who pass the nursery on their way to work but neither live nor work in the area. Here, you will need to consider:

• *whether you are near enough a commuting route to attract business from this market*

• *whether your location is accessible (for example, does a one-way system mean a short turn off the main road for parents in the morning but a long detour in the evening?)*

• *whether you will be able to communicate with this market. (Note that when you come to assess the viability of the three markets, you will need to consider how you will communicate with each, bearing in mind that it is harder to communicate with the commuting market. See Chapter 10: Marketing and customer care.)*

SOURCES OF INFORMATION

The information that you need for your market research can be gleaned in several ways:

Look around

There is no substitute for a good nosey around the locality. See if there is evidence of young families in the area. For example, are there a number of infant and junior schools, or a number of shops in the area catering for young children's needs? (Look out for Mothercare and Early Learning Centre.) Is the housing suitable for young families? Are there many day nurseries, and are they full? (See Competition, below.)

Childcare registration officers

Childcare registration officers within the local authority are a good source of information. They are aware of local childcare needs and can steer you towards other forms of market research. Ask for a copy of the local authority's standard list of nurseries and childminders to establish the competition. You will also need the local guidelines (these are the local interpretations of the Children Act 1989), which are usually free of charge but some authorities levy a fee. And it is worth requesting a copy of the early years development and childcare partnership plan, which sets out the plans for childcare locally. If you can, have a chat with the registration officers. In most cases they will be very helpful, but try to plan your questions first.

Employers

Nearby most nurseries, there will be employers such as hospitals, offices and colleges, and many will be in need of childcare for their employees. Contact any major employers to establish whether they have a need to provide childcare for their employees. (If you come to market your service to them, you will want to know if they would be interested in reserving places, or be prepared to publicise your nursery to their staff.) The main point of contact will be the personnel manager. Try to establish what, if any, childcare provisions they make for their staff and how many women are on maternity leave. You can also identify opportunities for marketing to them at a later date. (See Chapter 5: Workplace nurseries.)

Demographic profiles

Demographics are statistics covering the residential market, such as the number of under-fives in the areas and income per household. There are various sources of up-to-date information such as Experian (formerly CCN) and CACI. They will provide reports based on criteria that you select but these can be very costly. They are also able to provide information about the corporate market, such as the number of professionals working in the area and how they travel to work. Such figures are only useful if you can compare them with the same statistics from a successful nursery business.

The best sources for cheap demographic information are the local Training and Enterprise Councils (TECs) or Scottish equivalent, the Local Enterprise Councils (LECs), and Business Links, which provide links between potential funders and local entrepreneurs. The economic development department of your local authority should be able to provide a copy of its unitary development plan, which outlines business development for the area and includes such statistics as the number of working parents in the area. Chambers of commerce is a good source of business demographics and for a fee, they will provide local business information.

Commercial estate agents keep up-to-date demographic statistics to attract new business to the area. Residential estate agents are aware of new housing developments and, of course, the price of local housing can tell you a lot about an area.

Questionnaires

A useful exercise is to prepare your own market research questionnaire, arm yourself with a clipboard and conduct a survey at the shopping centre nearest to your proposed location. Questions to include in your questionnaire are:

- *What area do you live in?*

- *Do you work? If so, where?*

- *Do you have children under the age of five?*

- *Do you use any childcare at present? If so, does your current childcare meet your needs?*

- *What hours/days would you need childcare?*

- *Do both parents or carers in the family work?*

- *How much would you be prepared to pay for childcare?*

- *If a nursery were available locally would you like further information about it? (Use the opportunity to publicise your nursery and to take the addresses of interested parties, so that you can inform them about the opening date of your nursery.)*

If you think it is appropriate, bring along something for children, such as Helium-filled balloons, while conducting your survey. Parents may be more amenable to answering your questions if their children are temporarily entertained.

You could also prepare a questionnaire for hand delivery in residential areas where young families live. If you add a number of questions relating to the service that they would like to have available, then you can begin to structure the type of provision you will offer, based on a genuine need. Consider any of the elements of service you would think appropriate to offer and ask parents how important they think these elements are.

The National Childbirth Trust

The National Childbirth Trust (NCT) provides advice for parents and is another great source of information. You may be able to access its members through meetings and its local magazine. Make contact through the Trust's local secretary.

Competition

One of the best ways in which to determine the viability of your potential business is to look at the competition. Rival childcare providers are an excellent source of information.

It is important to establish what services they offer and how much they charge, but if you engage them in conversation you can often build up a clear picture of the quality and quantity of both demand and supply in the area.

Once you have conducted your research into the competition, it is useful to compile a competitor analysis. This report forms an important part of your market appraisal for your nursery (see below) and should be included in your business plan.

PRICE

The price you will charge will be one of the determining factors in the success of your business and one of the best ways in which to establish an appropriate fee level is to find out what the competition charge.

This does not mean that you should charge the same as your competitors, but it will give you a clear idea of what level of fees the local market currently sustains. (For further details about Price, see Chapter 10: Marketing and customer care.)

MARKET APPRAISAL

It is advisable to draw up a market appraisal of the childcare market based around your proposed location. Such an exercise will help you and potential lenders or business partners assess the viability of your nursery. The final appraisal should be incorporated into the market research section in your business plan. Use the fictitious sample below as a guide on how to present the information.

Marketing appraisal for a new day nursery in Handbridge, Chester

Index

1 *Background*

2 *Site information*

3 *Marketing Appraisal*

3.1 *Residential*

3.2 *Corporate*

1 Background

It is intended to develop a new 65-place day nursery in Handbridge, Chester. The nursery will offer childcare and education to children aged six weeks to five years, from Monday to Friday, 8.00am to 6.00pm, 52 weeks a year. This appraisal provides market research information for the nursery.

2 Site information

The nursery will be sited in Handbridge, Chester and is accessible from the A483, off the A55, the main southern ring road around Chester. At the site there is provision for 15 car-parking places.

3 Marketing appraisal

The market for nursery care falls into three parts: the residential, the corporate and the commuting.

3.1 Residential

With regard to the 'residential' market, the nursery will attract business from the local residential community of Handbridge. Over 1,000 homes have recently been built in the area and further development is planned. All of these homes fit in to the category of 'starter homes' for new families and will, therefore, be directly in the target market for childcare.

Demographics for the existing residential market show that there is a high penetration of children under four years old and parents are able to afford the childcare fees recommended below. At least 60 per cent of users are expected to come from the residential market.

3.2 Corporate

The 'corporate' market comprises the employers in Chester and tenants on the local business park. On the park, over 45,000m² of office space has been developed and planning consent has been granted for a further 60,000m².

Major businesses in the area, which are in the usual target market for childcare, include:

Company name	Number of employees
XYZ Ltd	300
ABC Ltd	450
MNO Ltd	580
Total	1,330

These companies have been consulted and on the basis of these discussions, the corporate market is expected to account for 15 to 20 per cent of the nursery's business.

3.3 Commuting

Handbridge is en route into Chester from the south and the nursery is located just off the A483, one of the main commuting routes into Chester. Commuters would not have to make a major detour from their journey to work in order to reach the nursery. It

is, therefore, assumed that the nursery will attract up to 20 per cent of its business from this market.

3.4 Demographic analysis

Market research reports show the residential area to fall within the target market for nursery care. There is a high number of 'nestmaking families' and the penetration of the target groups is 50 per cent above the average for the country.

3.5 Competitor analysis

COMPETITOR NURSERY*		MNO Nursery	ABC Nursery	XYZ Nursery
SIZE		80	50	42
AVAILABILITY OF PLACES		Full for under 3s Places for 3–5s	Full	Full
CURRENT PRICE PER WEEK £	0–2	125	120	118
	2–3	125	120	118
	3–5	115	100	100
PRICE INCLUSIVE OF:	Nappies	Yes	No	No
	Formulas	Yes	No	No
	Meals	Yes	Yes	Yes
HOURS OPEN		8am–6pm Mon to Fri	8am–5.30pm Mon to Fri	8.30am–5.30pm Mon to Fri
NOTES		Purpose-built, good reputation. Long waiting list	Converted church, good reputation	Old school, good reputation

Analysis based on a three-mile radius of proposed nursery

3.6 Price

Based on the competitor information alone, it is anticipated that the local market will support a fee level of £125 per week for babies and £115 per week for three- to five-year-olds. This price will be reviewed as occupancy develops.

4 Summary

There is potential for a new nursery in the proposed location as there is little competition in the area. Taking into account the anticipated fee level and occupancy rates, subject to marketing being conducted as per plan, it is expected that the turnover for the first three years will be as follows:

Year	Turnover £
Year 1	100,000
Year 2	200,000
Year 3	250,000

Appendices

These might include sample geodemographic reports; photographs of the area and of the proposed site; photographs of competitors' nurseries; corporate market information.

3: DRAWING UP A BUSINESS PLAN

IF YOU WANT TO MAKE THE SHIFT from employee to employer, you will need to start with a good business plan. It details what you are going to do and how you are going to do it, and it should demonstrate that you and your team have the skills required to be successful.

WHAT IS A BUSINESS PLAN?

A business plan is simply a document which shows how much money you will need to borrow in order to set up and operate your business. Its purpose is to demonstrate that your business proposition is viable and to convince others (and yourself) that you know what you are doing. It therefore needs to detail every aspect of your proposed business, from market research to staff recruitment and implementation plans (see 'The structure of the business plan', page 26). Most importantly, it needs to include a detailed 'financial trading model', in which you make all your predictions about how your nursery will develop.

THE FINANCIAL TRADING MODEL

Start your business plan with the financial trading model. This is a spreadsheet which shows predicted income and expenditure and the resulting profit/loss. It will serve to illustrate your nursery's performance over an imaginary year.

Although you might enlist the skills of an accountant to help with the number crunching and the presentation of your business plan, it is important that you do the bulk of the work yourself. Equally essential is a computer spreadsheet programme because you will want to alter figures to see how these changes affect profitability. A computer spreadsheet will enable you to answer questions like, 'If I increase fees by £1 per week, how much more can I pay my staff whilst retaining the same level of profitability?' or 'If I increase the number of baby places to 10, how will this affect staff costs?' So, if you don't have access to a computer, you should make that your first step.

Income

In your business plan, you will want to show income as the result of fees multiplied by occupancy. And you will need to bear in mind that the two factors are intrinsically linked, that is the fee level you impose will have a direct impact on your level of occupancy. Finding the optimum fee rate to achieve the highest level of income is a balancing act and you will need to exercise your judgement based on your market research and your own experience. Try to be as realistic as possible with income projections and always err on the side of caution (see opposite).

Expenditure

Expenditure should cover every aspect of nursery bills from staff to insurance (see opposite). You may wish to show expenditure split into two sections: expenditure which is dependent on the number of children, such as food and drink, (variable), and that which you have to pay anyway, regardless of child numbers, such as rent and rates (fixed).

Sample

When you set up your financial trading model you can estimate the growth of the business over time. To show the nursery's full potential, you should prepare your projections for income and expenditure and profit/loss for the first 12 months and thereafter until the nursery is full. Your financial trading model should include the information in the table opposite but the table it is not intended as a template. You should design your own to ensure that it fits your proposed business.

FINANCIAL TRADING MODEL	Month 1	Month 2	Month 3
Occupancy by month (no of places)	5	10	15
INCOME £			
Fees for under-twos			
Fees for two- to three-year-olds			
Fees for three-year-olds and over			
Other income, for example, afterschool care			
EXPENDITURE £			
Staff			
Salaries			
National Insurance			
Recruitment and training			
Agency staff			
Premises			
Rent and rates			
Heat and light			
Gardening			
Insurance			
Maintenance			
Equipment			
Cleaning and materials			
Child costs			
Food and drink			
Milks/formulas			
Nappies			
Chemist purchases			
Trips			
Small equipment			
Consumables eg paint and paper			
Administrative and financial			
Telephone			
Office costs			
Accountancy			
Legal			
Bank charges			
Debt repayment			
Marketing			
Travel			
Depreciation			
Irrecoverable VAT			
PROFIT/LOSS			

PROFIT AND LOSS ACCOUNT

Most investors will look first to the Profit & Loss Account (P&L), which summarises the performance of the business year on year and should cover three to five years' trading. (It will be necessary to show three to five years, because the business is unlikely to be making much money until at least the second year.)

The sample P&L below is based on a company opening three medium-to-large nurseries in reasonably affluent areas, over three years and then consolidating its position (so not opening any further nurseries).

The figures are based on several assumptions, including:

* *all three premises are leased*

* *most of the investment comes from equity capital and the remainder from loan capital (see Chapter 6: Funding options)*

* *the owner takes a reasonably modest salary*

GREENHOUSE NURSERIES — SAMPLE PROFIT AND LOSS ACCOUNT								
	Year 1 £		Year 2 £		Year 3 £		Year 4 £	
Nursery	Turnover	Profit	Turnover	Profit	Turnover	Profit	Turnover	Profit
Greenhouse 1	252,333	11,344	336,057	48,776	382,191	87,034	382,191	87,034
Greenhouse 2			271,377	18,776	360,555	63,112	360,555	63,112
Greenhouse 3					162,443	-6,034	162,443	-6,034
Total	**252,333**	**11,344**	**607,434**	**67,552**	**905,189**	**144,112**	**905,189**	**144,112**
Admin costs		33,779		53,880		62,340		62,340
Net operating profit/(loss)		**(22,435)**		**13,672**		**81,772**		**81,772**
Less capital repayments		4,125		9,350		14,760		14,760
Total operating profit/(loss)		**£26,560**		**£4,322**		**£67,012**		**£67,012**

Cash flow projection

Once the financial trading model is set up to show a year's trading, you will need to show the timing of income and expenditure, month on month. The resulting cash flow projection will demonstrate how much you will need to borrow and when to borrow it to keep the business afloat.

There will be many costs associated with the business which are incurred before trading or in the early months and the cash flow will need to take account of these initial costs (see below).

CHECKLIST OF INITIAL COSTS

Premises

You may have selected the premises you are seeking to rent and established the level of rent and the lease terms with the landlord, or at this stage you may just have some idea of costs. You are unlikely to find premises ready for use as a nursery so you will need to establish the costs of fitting out the premises as a nursery and include them in the financial model. Other premises related costs include insurance and the fee for nursery registration, carried out by the local authority.

Equipment

You should have selected the equipment for your nursery and have added the cost of the equipment list to your plan.

Staff

Before opening you will need to ensure that you have a well-inducted core staff team. So, you will need to budget for pre-opening staff costs including recruitment, salaries and training.

Marketing

You will need to ensure that you budget for marketing costs, such as signage, advertising and PR.

Trading losses

Most nurseries lose money before they reach 55 to 65 per cent occupancy so you will need to allow for early trading losses in your budgeting.

Once you have prepared the financial information you can write up the text to support and explain the trading model in detail. Ensure that the information is in a presentable format as in the suggested structure below.

THE STRUCTURE OF THE BUSINESS PLAN

Executive summary
A two-page summary including details of:

- *key objectives*

- *three- to five-year financial objectives*

- *level of funding needed*

- *management team*

- *benefits to potential funders*

- *the status of the project (that is, where you are up to)*

Background/the nursery marketplace
This should include a brief explanation of the nursery sector and trends within it, such as the growing numbers of women returning to work after childbirth. (Note that not all potential funders will know the nursery business like you do.)

Market research
Specific information about your nursery and where your customers will come from. You may wish to write this as a market appraisal (see Chapter 2: Market research).

Operational plan
Start with the key business objectives such as what you expect to achieve and by when. The operational plan should then give an explanation of how you expect to achieve those objectives by showing how the business will operate and should detail:

- *ethos*

- *opening hours*

- *age groups*

- *premises*

- *management controls to ensure the delivery of quality practice – policies such as health and safety, food policy, parental involvement, procedures and curriculum. (Keep the details of the policies for the Appendix.)*

Management team

This is your chance to sing your praises as a manager. Include any people you have identified in order for the business to succeed and the timing of their recruitment. You would be advised to include, if possible, a diagram showing the management structure.

Implementation plan

This is the critical path to opening and should include all the steps you will take during the start-up phase. You might include :

- *securing premises and equipment*

- *liaising with regulatory authorities*

- *staff recruitment and induction*

- *marketing (include your pre-opening plan here or in the marketing plan)*

Marketing plan

This section should detail marketing plans for the business based on the information you have gathered during market research. Include methods such as advertising and signage. Explain what makes your business different and how you intend to inform potential customers about the nursery. Explain how you have arrived at the fee level.

Include some element of risk analysis to show that you have considered what could go wrong and how to deal with it, for example, if occupancy rates are lower than anticipated or if you face a staff recruitment crisis.

Financial information

The financial information details all your predictions about how your nursery will develop financially. It includes your financial trading model, a cash flow analysis and a three- to five-year profit and loss account. If you need help with this section, seek the advice of an accountant.

Appendices
This section provides more detailed information which people can refer to but would detract from the main points in the rest of the plan, for example:

- *your CV and those of your management team*

- *market research details*

- *magazine or newspaper articles about the nursery sector*

- *policies and practice, including the curriculum*

Anyone will tell you that no matter how much you try, things never quite turn out as planned. So, one thing to accept about the business plan is that it is never really finished and it should keep changing as your ideas are modified.

4: BUYING A NURSERY

ACQUIRING SUITABLE NURSERY PREMISES can be a slow process and you then have to find your own staff and customers. So are you better off taking a short cut and buying an existing nursery business, which gives you an income stream from day one? Only if you are aware of the challenges, as well as the benefits, of this route into business.

BUYING – THE BENEFITS

At any time there may be 200 or more nurseries for sale in the UK and many more considering selling. As a potential operator, you could buy one of these existing businesses and be up and

running much more rapidly than if you had set up your own nursery from scratch.

Clearly, an immediate income stream has its benefits. To find a nursery that you are happy to make your own may take as long, or even longer, as finding premises, but on the day of exchange of contracts, you will be trading and in profit (provided you have bought a profitable nursery).

The nursery staff team will come with years of experience of working in childcare. Inheriting expertise is particularly useful if you plan to open further nurseries, because it gives your company some management infrastructure from which to grow.

The staff should also know the procedures and policies of the nursery intimately, which may give you the opportunity to ease into the business gently. If the previous owner has been 'hands off' for a while, perhaps in semi-retirement, then the existing manager or supervisor may have gained enough autonomy to be able to deal with the day-to-day operation efficiently, leaving you free to focus on any improvements. Of course, procedures and policies should be in place, which will save time having to devise and document them.

You will have access to the trading accounts of the business you are buying, and with these figures, it may be easier to secure a loan than if you were starting your own nursery, provided you can demonstrate that you have negotiated a good deal. You will need to show that there is enough financial 'cover', that is that the profits are substantial enough to cover the interest repayments and leave a comfortable margin of error. Many banks will look on a takeover as a continuation of the existing trading position and you will need to illustrate how your improvements will enhance profitability.

Taking over the right nursery and making changes slowly can lead to success. It may take a few years before you arrive at the nursery of your dreams, but you will have had the benefit of those years of profitability.

BUYING – THE PITFALLS

You will need to ensure that you are comfortable as to why the current owner is parting with the business. Retirement tends to be the most frequent reason for selling a nursery business but be wary of other motives in case they disguise a poor operation or reputation.

Other than your own assessment, Office for Standards in Education (Ofsted) and social services reports will give you an idea of the nursery's reputation, but try also to speak to parents, the local authority childcare registration officer and even competitors if you can. You will be able to advertise the fact that the nursery is under new management but it will still take time and effort if you have to turn round a poor reputation.

You would also be advised to look closely at any nursery where the owner is still very actively involved in the day-to-day running of the business. Unless the owner has delegated and built up the skills of the staff team, you may find that a 'tight ship' quickly begins to founder once the 'captain' is no longer at the helm.

Another factor for consideration is the price. In a buoyant market, the laws of supply and demand dictate that you may pay over the odds for a nursery business, particularly if there are several new entrants keen to get a foothold in the sector. If nursery values rise inexorably, then it will not matter, but you will want to be wary of buying at a high price at the wrong time.

Likewise, be cautious over the amount you pay for goodwill (that is, the existing and potential customers and the income that comes from them). Where owners have put many years' hard work into the business and generated a lot of happy, loyal parents, children and staff, they will naturally expect to achieve a high price for goodwill. However, if after your takeover, problems arise and parents take their children out of the nursery, you stand to lose the money you paid for those customers. You will need to ensure that your business benefits from any goodwill bought.

It is the experience of many potential buyers that an owner may be in two minds about selling, despite appearing committed to the sale. As a result, you could find yourself close to completing a purchase, having spent money on a valuation, legal fees and possibly accountancy fees, only to find that the owner has a last minute change of heart. Occasionally owners put their nurseries on the market simply to ascertain the value of their business, so as a prospective buyer you could be unlucky enough to find your time being wasted. In addition, if owners know that you are very keen to buy their nursery, then they will be able to determine the pace of the purchase, which can be frustrating.

When buying a nursery, a climate of concern can develop unless staff concerns about their jobs are handled sensitively. From the moment you know the sale will go ahead, spend time and effort reassuring them of the security of their position. Explain your plans in detail and canvass opinion regarding possible improvements to the nursery. Listen to their views – as with all good management, the more you listen, the more you will gain their respect. The staff with the best grasp of how and what to improve are usually those directly involved in hands-on childcare.

Any changes must be introduced gradually and only after consulting parents. Childcare can be an emotive issue and many parents, who make childcare choices based on the factors at the time, can be highly resistant to change. Working in partnership with them is essential to the success of your business. By rushing ahead with changes and without any consultation, you run the risk of meeting strong opposition. The staff may be equally resistant to change unless this too is handled sensitively.

You may find staff justifying their actions ('...but we have always done it like that'). To change any bad practice, you will have to demonstrate considerable tact and accept that the process will be slow. In fact, breaking bad habits can be more work than establishing good practice in a brand new nursery (see Chapter 11: Management and staffing).

Summary

Benefits

- *Buying enables you to open for business sooner than if you start a nursery from scratch*

- *It gives you an immediate income stream*

- *You inherit expertise, policies, procedures, equipment, and so on*

- *It may be easier to borrow capital*

Pitfalls of buying a nursery

- *You may pay for goodwill from which you do not benefit*

- *You will need to listen to staff and parents and have considerable tact*

- *The organisation may collapse when the owner leaves*

- *Changes will need to be introduced slowly*

- *You could face abortive costs, wasted time or be frustrated*

- *You may inherit a poor reputation which is hard to shake*

- *You may pay more than the nursery is worth if the market is buoyant*

PROPERTIES FOR SALE

Where do you find these 200 nurseries that may be for sale? Well, there are various reliable sources with considerable experience in the nursery sector and the best established are A H Lansley, National School Transfer and School Transfer Consultants.

These three companies advertise regularly in *Nursery World* and often list a few samples of what they have in their portfolio. Christie & Co, local agents and business consultants, also handle nursery sales. You can always approach a nursery directly if you like the look of it, but you will need to be tactful and the price may inflate if the owner does not need to sell but can see how interested you are in buying.

For vendors, the agents charge a commission but as a 'searcher' you will simply need to register (National School Transfer charges a £10 registration fee). However, the company will need convincing that you are a genuine buyer.

The agents will provide a list, summarising the nurseries they have for sale. They tend to give little detail beyond what is necessary as they need to protect the confidentiality of their vendors. They will offer nurseries in both freehold and leasehold premises all over the country from as little as £20,000. As with any purchase, you tend to get what you pay for. Your financial backing will probably determine whether you pursue a freehold or a leasehold purchase.

VALUATION

You will need to make an offer for the nursery you select based on what you can afford to pay and what you judge to be a reasonable price. There are many different methods by which to make your valuation and many variables to take into consideration.

If your funding is from a bank, then they are likely to lend up to 75 per cent of an independent valuation of the nursery (regardless of whether it is different from your offer price). The process is similar to arranging a house mortgage although the term of the loan tends to be up to a maximum of 15 years. You will have to find the remainder from a separate source, such as through an equity partner (see Chapter 6: Funding options). For example:

Greenhouse Nursery

Offer price for Greenhouse Nursery	£650,000
Independent valuation of Greenhouse Nursery	£635,000
Bank lending at 75 per cent of valuation	£476,250
Equity capital needed	£173,750
Total	**£650,000**

OFFER PRICE

There are various ways to arrive at a sensible offer price for the nursery. The examples below – they are intended as illustrations only – refer to a 72-place freehold nursery and the freehold value of the propery (including any land) is assumed to be £440,000.

Multiples of earnings

A commercial bank will commission a valuer to establish a value, usually based on a multiple of Earnings Before Interest payments, Tax and Depreciation (EBITD). In the childcare sector a standard multiple has not been clearly established but many freehold nurseries sold in recent years have averaged a multiple of between four and six. For example:

Greenhouse Nursery

Gross income	£340,000
Total costs	£210,000
Profit before bank interest, tax and depreciation	£130,000
Valuation of freehold, goodwill, fixtures and fittings, based on a multiple of five times profit	£650,000
Freehold value alone	£440,000
Weekly fee	£125

Multiples of earnings and freehold value

In the case of a freehold nursery, a valuer may also consider it appropriate to take into account the value of the land and building/s. A multiple would then apply to the trading element of the business. Again, no standard has clearly been established but multiples of between one and 2.5 of the trading element currently apply in the sector. For example:

Greenhouse Nursery

Gross income	£340,000
Total costs	£210,000
Profit before bank interest, tax and depreciation	£130,000
Valuation of profits of the business based on a multiple of 1.62	£210,000
Freehold value alone	£440,000
Joint valuation of freehold and profit	£650,000
Weekly fee	£125

Price per place

Another measurement of sale value is price per place. Most freehold nurseries sold in recent years have achieved between £7,000 and £10,000 per place. For example:

Greenhouse Nursery

Gross income	£340,000
Total costs	£210,000
Profit before bank interest, tax and depreciation	£130,000
Valuation of nursery based on price per place of £9000	£650,000
Freehold value alone	£440,000
Weekly fee	£125

The price per place measurement alone does not take into account the fact that a fee per place of £125 per week will offer greater value to you than a fee level of £100 per week. To make a comparison, you can create your own index by dividing the weekly fee by the price per place and multiplying it by 100. For example:

Nurseries visited	Weekly fee £	Price per place £	Index
Greenhouse Nursery	125	£9,000	1.39
Another Nursery	100	£9,000	1.11

The higher the index, the better value the acquisition. Thus, despite having the same price per place, the Greenhouse Nursery offers better value as a purchase than Another Nursery.

What can you afford?

Whatever the multiple acceptable to your lender, or the price per place index, you will only be able to pay what you can afford. Once the level of interest payable on your loan capital has been established (for example, 2.5 per cent above base rate), put all the known variables of the business for sale into the financial trading model in your business plan, which should then indicate the price you can afford (see Chapter 3: Drawing up a business plan).

What are you prepared to pay?

It can be useful to conduct an exercise that demonstrates what you would have to spend to arrive at the trading position of the nursery for sale. Assume that you were to start from scratch, add the combined costs of the building, staff recruitment, equipment, marketing, trading losses, time and so on, then make an allowance for depreciation and the costs of making improvements. This should establish a maximum price you would be prepared to pay.

Additional costs

There are various costs to take into consideration in addition to the purchase price. Try to establish the level of these fees before committing yourself to the purchase. Additional costs include valuation of the nursery, stamp duty (if freehold), solicitor's fees, accountant's fees and any irrecoverable VAT.

ACQUISITION

Once your offer has been accepted, you will need to start the process of buying the nursery, which involves getting to know exactly what you are buying (although the truth is you will not really know until you have bought it).

When buying any nursery, what you are seeking to acquire is the building (leased or freehold), the equipment the staff and the children and the potential business which may arise from the good reputation. It is advisable to pursue the shortest and simplest route to achieve that which means the purchase of the assets only.

The acquisition may involve taking over a limited company or just buying assets. In many cases, nurseries are operated as 'sole traders' or 'partnerships' rather than as limited companies and if this is the case regarding your acquisition, then you will be simply purchasing assets. With a limited company, the liabilities (money the business owes) are limited to the shareholders and if you buy the company you take on any liabilities. A limited company acquisition is not uncommon in the nursery sector and requires more care.

Buying a limited company

If the nursery for sale is operated by a limited company and the vendor determines that you must buy that company, then you

will need to conduct a process of 'due diligence' which ensures you do not take on any potential liabilities. That process may take some time and should involve an accountant with the appropriate experience.

If your accountant or solicitor advises you to pursue an asset purchase instead, then you may wish to try to negotiate with the owner to purchase the assets from the limited company, leaving them with an empty 'shell' company. This is worth consideration and you should seek advice. Suffice to say it can cost more and take longer to acquire a limited company than to buy assets.

Whether buying a limited company or a sole trader (or partnership) company, you will still need to pursue a process of due diligence.

Buying process
The first step is to instruct your solicitors that you intend to make the acquisition. They will contact the vendor's solicitors and confirm that they have both been instructed. Your solicitor

will be needed to advise you regarding the purchaser's agreement, which the vendor's solicitor should prepare. This agreement is the 'contract' and it details what is included in the sale. It can also incorporate any provisions you like, as long as they are agreed. For example, you may wish to add an anti-competition proviso prohibiting the vendor from setting up another nursery locally, or preventing them from approaching your staff.

If the purchase involves a leasehold nursery, your solicitor will need to consider the terms of the lease and advise you. You may even wish to contact the landlord and try to renegotiate terms. If the property is freehold your solicitor will need to establish secure 'Title' (that is that the vendor owns the property and land unencumbered) and they will conduct the usual searches on your behalf.

An independent valuation is likely to be needed to convince your lender that the purchase price matches the true value. There are a number of valuers with experience in this sector such as Taylors, Pinders and Chestertons but the choice will probably be determined by your lender and you will bear the cost. The valuer will prepare a comprehensive document and you should request a copy.

The vendor will need to provide a considerable volume of information and it is worth discussing this with them before the acquisition in order to structure their expectations. They need to understand that the process of selling the nursery will involve hard work for them. The key information you will require is outlined opposite, along with some reminders:

TAKEOVER CHECKLIST

Before the takeover

- Make sure you have:
- – details of salaries, terms and conditions, qualifications and length of service
- – occupancy figures for each session and a list of all parents
- – fee levels, payment methods and money held on deposit
- – list of all suppliers and the terms on which they supply
- – lease terms, or title deeds, if freehold
- – floor plans and photos of the nursery
- – last three years' accounts and trading account with projections
- Meet staff and reassure them
- Meet parents and reassure them

On takeover

- Make sure you have arranged:
- – to take over the fee payment system
- – to take over the salary/payroll system
- – to pay bills (gas and electric, rates, telephone, deliveries, service contracts, hire purchase agreements and other payments such as subscriptions)
- – insurances
- Register the nursery in a new name and ensure compliance including procedures and staff (for example, qualifications)

After takeover

- Consider:
- – replacing the stationery
- – introducing induction and training plans
- – planning and budgeting for redecoration or improvements
- – future marketing plans

5: WORKPLACE NURSERIES

EMPLOYERS SEEKING TO ATTRACT **and retain employees frequently consider providing a nursery for their staff's children. These employers invariably use the expertise of established childcare operators to run the nursery. A workplace nursery, therefore, can offer a potential start-up route for a new operator, but with no track record, you will need good contacts and an effective sales campaign.**

THE MARKETPLACE

Within the nursery sector, there is an area of activity that can be defined as the workplace nursery marketplace.

Since the mid-1980s, increasing numbers of employers have started providing childcare as a service for staff. The trend has been in response to worsening problems faced by companies in finding and retaining skilled employees. One of the companies to take the lead in providing childcare was Midland Bank (now HSBC). It was concerned by the high numbers of women who had decided against returning to work after maternity leave and the damaging affect this was having on business[1]. In response, the company devised a childcare strategy, which involved the bank entering into 'partnerships' all over the country with existing childcare operators to provide childcare places for its employees. By 1997 Midland staff had taken over 900 places in partnership nurseries. The company later set up a small number of their own nurseries, managed by an experienced operator.

Around the same time that Midland Bank and others were considering childcare for staff, the need for childcare was acknowledged by the Government in the Income and Corporation Taxes Act 1988, which allowed employers to provide childcare free of charge to employees, without the employee

[1] This rate of non-return for Midland Bank maternity leavers in 1988 was 70 per cent

attracting tax as a benefit in kind. However, very few employers have been prepared to bear the entire cost of childcare for their staff's children[1].

Yet today there are many employers who have reaped the benefits of childcare provision for staff. The main benefits to the employer are:

- *Recruitment costs fall as staff turnover rates decrease*

- *Women on maternity leave are more likely to return*

- *Investment in staff training and development is recouped*

- *Employee morale improves and stress rates fall*

- *Employees are more able to balance work and home commitments*

- *There is a reduction in absentee rates*

- *The employer can draw on a wider pool of potential recruits for jobs, including parents of young children*

- *The employer is acknowledged as valuing staff*

- *By acknowledging its social responsibilities, the employer benefits from public recognition*

However, for the employer, the provision of childcare is not without its problems. Most employers agree that it is important to provide high quality childcare, and in acknowledgement of the fact that a bank or a pharmaceutical company is not in the business of childcare, they seek the expertise of well-established operators.

Most of the workplace nurseries that exist today have been originated and funded by the employer and tend to be on or very near the place of employment. The employer will put up the capital to fund the construction of the nursery, charge parents for its use and the day-to-day running of the nursery is then

[1] The Treasury has always resisted calls for company tax breaks on providing childcare and for employees to claim childcare as a tax-deductible expense. Instead, the Government has opted to introduce a Working Families Tax Credit, which includes the Childcare Tax Credit. The Credit will benefit only low and medium-income families and will be administered through the payroll

contracted to an operator. If the project is not financially self-sufficient and needs to be subsidised, then this cost is borne by the employer and can be described as the 'risk' of the venture.

In recent years it has become harder to define the difference between a 'workplace' nursery operated for an employer and a private day nursery. This is because the relationship between the 'employer' and 'operator' has changed as the balance of 'risk' has shifted.

PROVISION

There are several ways in which the employer can provide childcare:

Management fee

The employer provides the premises and equipment and a budget for operating the nursery and pays the nursery operator a fixed management fee for the service. The operator employs the staff, operates within the budget and collects the childcare fees on behalf of the employer. The contract is usually for a fixed term, say three to five years, enabling the employer to re-tender at the end of the period if necessary.

Although these contracts are still very much the norm, it is becoming increasingly common for both parties to share the risk of the venture.

Shared risk

The employer provides the premises and equipment. The operator runs the nursery as if it were the owner, often on a leasehold basis from the employer. The operator collects fees from the employees as payment for the service. The contract usually covers a fixed period, often longer than that for a management fee contract. If the viability of the nursery is in question when run on this basis, then there are several options which can be agreed between operator and employer. The two most likely are:

- *The operator is also able to sell places to 'external users', that is local residents or other employees not working for the employer. These places can often be charged at a higher rate*
- *The employer agrees to 'cap' the risk for the operator by guaranteeing an acceptable level of financial return*

Joint venture

The employer and operator both put capital into the project and then run the nursery on a shared risk basis, as above. The operator is then able to agree a longer period under the contract with the employer, to ensure that the capital invested is recouped through the return in profit.

Contracting in

More recently, a fourth method has found favour with both operator and employer. It is this method of provision which has begun to blur the distinction between the private day nursery and the workplace nursery.

In this instance, the operator seeks out an employer with a childcare need and then takes all the risk of constructing or converting a nursery near the employer's workplace. Before committing any capital, the operator consults with the employer and agrees by contract that once the facility is ready the employer will take a number of places in the nursery.

There are benefits to both sides in this transaction. The employer has no need to set aside capital for a venture for which the risk is hard to measure. The operator has more control by not having to re-tender for a workplace contract and can offset initial trading losses in the nursery by virtue of the fact that some places are already paid for from day one.

In each of these cases, the employer may elect to subsidise the places to employees so that a larger percentage of their workforce can take advantage of the service[2]. In many workplace nurseries a 25 per cent subsidy of the cost of childcare can increase access to the service from 30 per cent of all staff to 60 per cent.

OPPORTUNITIES

As a new operator, entering into a contract with an employer to provide a workplace nursery service offers a low-cost route to starting up in business. Realistically, a few factors need to be in place to increase the chances of success.

Firstly, you would need to be able to convince an employer that you or your team have considerable experience in childcare and that you have a reasonable understanding of how the day-to-day operation of a workplace nursery differs from that of a private day nursery.

Secondly, as you progress in your negotiations with an employer, you will be involved in detailed discussion about the workplace contract, and you will need some experience of negotiating such contracts.

Thirdly, to stand any chance of succeeding, you will need to identify a potential client and build a relationship with that client.

Workplace nurseries are frequently tendered in *Nursery World* and you could respond to those tenders, but as a would-be nursery operator, the chances of securing a contract through the

2 One of the more interesting schemes is operated by The Body Shop at its Littlehampton nursery, where employees' childcare fees are charged on a percentage of salary basis

tendering route are very slim. It is likely that all employers operating a formal tender system will be looking for considerable experience of operating a workplace nursery and you will have to compete with the established workplace operators such as Kinderquest, Busy Bees and Kids Unlimited.

You would probably need to be able to display the quality of your service by taking the decision-makers to one of your existing nurseries and if you do not yet have one, then you are a non-starter. In addition, because of the competition, the profit for the operator from a contract issued by tender is likely to be small.

The best way into the workplace market for new operators is by approaching employers that you know have a childcare need and selling your service to them. Without existing contacts of this type, you will need to start prospecting for business by narrowing down the potential clients and identifying target employers. This process of targeting employers to establish a childcare need and then convincing them that you can meet that need may be described as a 'sales campaign'.

SELLING YOUR SERVICE

Any sales campaign is high-risk because it can be very time consuming and there are no guarantees that you will find a customer. However, you will improve your chances if you target companies or institutions that employ large numbers of women and operate in a competitive market for staff. The main categories are:

- *banks, insurance and financial institutions*
- *large pharmaceutical companies*
- *universities and colleges*
- *technology and IT companies*
- *companies with large research and development teams*
- *utility companies*

- *hospitals*
- *large Government departments*
- *telephone-based service operations*

Track them down using Yellow Pages.

Prospecting for business

The next step towards securing some business should be a fact-finding phone call. Talk to the human resources managers in the companies you are targeting to establish:

- *how many employees they have*
- *the percentage of women employees*
- *how many staff are on maternity leave*
- *whether they have a childcare need*
- *what they provide for staff by way of childcare support at present*
- *if childcare has been discussed in the past and what options have been considered*
- *the name of the human resources director and anyone else who may be responsible for considering this issue*

Once you have identified employers that have a requirement for childcare, write to them requesting a brief meeting, outlining how you can help them meet their needs. Include any brochure you may have produced and make sure you look professional by writing on your own letter-headed paper.

If they agree to meet you, then this will be your big sales opportunity. Selling is all about meeting someone's needs. You will want to ensure, therefore, that the whole conversation is geared around meeting their childcare needs. At the end of the meeting, if you find that there is nothing in it for you, then walk away and start again. If you go to the meeting expecting the employer to simply set you up in business, then you will probably not get very far. Listen carefully and see if you can find a compromise that works for both parties.

From a start-up position, it is only through established contacts and a relationship-building exercise that you will be able to secure a workplace-type contract. You will need to ensure that once you have convinced a company to have a workplace nursery that the employer uses your services rather than goes to tender, and that will rely on the strength of your relationship.

6: FUNDING OPTIONS

FINDING THE BEST SOURCE OF FINANCE **to start a nursery can be a difficult process, but if you organise yourself you will succeed, although it may take some time. There are a number of steps that can make the process easier and should enable you to choose the most appropriate route.**

TYPES OF FUNDING

Firstly, you will need to decide what you are going to spend the money on, as this will affect what type of funding to use. For example, you may seek one source of funding if you intend to build a nursery and another source if you plan to rent premises. The option most new nursery operators favour is renting a property although historically many nurseries began in the ground floor of the proprietor's home. Whether you are buying a building or renting, as with any business, adequate funding is essential and there are a variety of sources you can pursue.

Before you can discuss your plans effectively with potential funders, you will need to work out how much money the business will need and include all the information in the financial trading model in your business plan (see Chapter 3: Drawing up a business plan). Once you have completed your budgeting and incorporated all the costs into the plan, you will be ready to discuss your requirements with potential funders. So, where do you start?

There are two main types of funding to consider, debt (or loan capital, which you borrow from a lender such as a High Street bank) and equity, which means selling a share in your business to a business partner, even though it has not yet begun trading. Both types of funding have advantages and disadvantages and

you will need to consider them carefully before deciding which is better for you.

Debt

Anyone who is prepared to lend you money as debt will consider the risk against the potential return on their investment. If you are able to put up collateral or security (for example, offering a charge on your home or other asset), then a lender is more likely to look upon the loan favourably as this arrangement increases the risk for you, while reducing the risk to them.

Once you have entered into a loan agreement, you will have to meet the repayments whether the nursery is in profit or not. If you are unable to do so, then the future of your business is uncertain. However, when you borrow the money, it should be at an affordable repayment rate and will be based on your financial trading models. So, if your financial trading models are accurate, your business should be fine (see Chapter 3: Drawing up a business plan).

The debt option allows you to retain ownership, so if you sell your nursery in the future, the full value of the business will be yours. You will also have full control of the business, so decision making will be your responsibility, and there will no requirement to refer to others, unless you choose to.

Debt also has the advantage of being quicker to implement than equity funding as the decision about whether to lend you money or not is made on largely financial criteria and the process of judging these is usually quite straightforward. With equity funding, you and the equity partner need to establish a relationship and feel confident that you can work together before making any commitments to invest, and this can take much longer.

Equity
Perhaps the most important benefit of equity finance is the fact that you will only be required to pay back your funder out of profits. Consequently, the company is safer from premature closure because the business will not have to bear the burden of making additional payments to your equity partner until it becomes profitable.

Your equity partner is also likely to get involved in the business, which may bring new skills. If you have a mix of equity and debt, your debt lender will want to see that the governance arrangements for the company are satisfactory. The skills and experience of the management team are sometimes referred to as the 'management covenant' of the company and a lender will feel more comfortable with the skills of your partner on board.

However, you will be surrendering some of the eventual profits of the business and the greater the risk on the side of your equity partner, the greater the expectation in terms of his or her reward. Therefore, to achieve a significant return on their investment, investors may seek a substantial share in the company.

This arrangement also requires you to give up some of control of the company to your partner, and you will both need to work efficiently with each other for the benefit of the business. Any equity partner relationship is something of a marriage and, like any marriage, it will involve a courtship period, during which time you will both want to be absolutely sure that you can work well together. Many businesses have found themselves in difficulty once they are trading because, having invested so much time, the partners have then been reluctant to acknowledge that their relationship is not ideal.

A further benefit of taking on equity funds is that it can increase the debt capacity of the company (that is it may unlock further finance from other partners or lenders).

It is usual for most businesses to operate with a mix of debt and equity and your preferences and financial circumstances will determine the balance between the two. You would be well advised to pursue both sources simultaneously and there are several potential sources for both types of funding.

DEBT FUNDING

Family and friends
The easiest and quickest source of debt is through family and friends. Many successful businesses have started in this way, so if you know someone with enough capital, do not be afraid to discuss your proposal and to show them your business plan. (Note that family and friends may also expect a share in the business, which would then become equity funding.)

Banks
A High Street bank may be in a position to consider lending money in the form of a loan or overdraft if you already have some capital or assets of your own.

Brokers and commercial banks
If you are looking to borrow a large sum of money (that is over £250,000), there are brokers who will approach the commercial banks for business funding and they can bring their contacts, experience and presentation skills to bear on your application. They will also handle the time-consuming aspects involved in

securing this kind of funding, such is the constant liaison that is required. A good broker can add considerable credibility to your proposal simply by virtue of their involvement. Ask your accountant to recommend one to you. You may approach commercial banks direct and they will consider your proposal if the value of the deal is substantial enough for them.

Grants

Grants are another source of funding with the advantage that they do not need to be repaid, but the sources are few. If you are under the age of 30, The Prince's Youth Business Trust is a good place to start. Your bank manager or local Training and Enterprise Council (Local Enterprise Council in Scotland) should be able to offer advice on how to source grants and will provide information about local schemes aimed at supporting new businesses.

Other lenders

Be cautious about approaching any other form of lenders and make sure that you take legal advice before giving any lender a charge over any of your assets.

Notes

• *Any source of debt funding will require monthly payments of capital and interest although you may be able to negotiate a period during which you pay only the interest until the business is up and running*

• *You are likely to pay a small arrangement fee and the lender will want some security, such as the ability to claim the assets of the company*

• *You will also be required to provide management figures and annual audited accounts*

• *Once you have a reliable trading record, you may be able to go back to your funder and request improved terms*

EQUITY FUNDING

Venture capital

Venture Capital companies (VCs) exist to provide funds for business. However, it is unlikely that a venture capital company will fund your new business unless you can convince them that you are going for considerable growth, or you are buying another nursery[1]. Because lending on a new business is high risk, venture capital companies look for a substantial return on their money and it is common for them to expect to double their money over a three-year period. This translates into a 25 per cent Internal Rate of Return (IRR) over a three-year investment.

They will always be considering how to 'realise' their investment in the company and this may include selling it. They are also only likely to get involved if the deal is big enough to merit their time. Most VCs will not look at deals where their investment is less than £250,000 and many look to invest considerably larger sums. All the active companies are listed in The British Venture Capital Association Directory, but it is worth discussing any approach to a VC with an accountant first.

Business angels

For a smaller start-up business, the best source of equity finance

[1] Buying another nursery can be deemed to be a Management Buy-in (MBI) (see Chapter 4: Buying a nursery)

is a business angel. There is no typical business angel, however let's break the rules and describe one. He (and it is more often a he) is likely to be over 50, with business experience, usually in senior management in a large company, possibly in a financial role, has a sum of money to invest and is keen to become involved in a profitable business. He may also wish to work with the business on a part-time basis bringing new skills to bear and keeping an eye on his investment at the same time.

There are an estimated 8,000 business angels with active investments of over £500m per year in over 3,500 business in the UK[2], and they keep their ear to the ground for new investments through a network of contacts. For a fee, you should be able to access those networks through either the local Training and Enterprise Council, Business Link, or through private agencies (their fees range from about £350 upward and your local TEC should be able to give you names). The TEC or agency will circulate a précis of your business plan in a newsletter and you may be given the opportunity to present your case to a group of potential investors.

Notes

• *The process of taking on an equity partner can take several months*

• *You will need to be sympathetic to their needs in order that your negotiations maintain a balance*

• *How big a share of your business to part with is usually an emotive issue and there are no set rules. If you feel comfortable with the deal, then that is the best you can expect. You will be the*

2 Richard Harrison, University of Ulster, Techinvest Seminar (January 1999)

one getting up at 6.30am to make sure the nursery is open on time, so you will need to feel motivated, and if you are unhappy with the deal, the business will suffer

APPROACHING LENDERS

Potential funders will want to see that you have shown an understanding of their needs, so that by the time you approach them, you should have all the information necessary for them to make a decision. The information will, therefore, need to include your business plan, details of your management team and proposals about how the shares in the company will be allocated.

You can discover a lot, particularly the jargon that surrounds investment, from talking to people who have dealt with funders before. Talk to business people whenever the opportunity arises. Ask them how they started, what funding they needed and how they attracted it and ask them to explain the meaning of any words you do not understand.

Be persistent. To secure funding, you will have to sell the idea of your business to funders and it will probably be the biggest 'sale' you will ever make.

7: PREMISES

ONE OF THE MOST DIFFICULT ASPECTS of starting your own nursery is acquiring suitable premises and each step of the way needs to be carefully planned (see timetable, page 70). First, you will need to give some consideration as to what sort of premises you are looking for.

PREMISES AND YOUR BUSINESS PLAN

One of the chicken-and-egg aspects of setting up an nursery is that many funders prefer to consider a tangible proposition before they agree to fund your business proposal – that is they want to see the actual premises from which you are planning to operate along with real costs. However, when you find suitable premises you will not wish to risk losing them by beginning the process of securing finance. It is, therefore, important to include assumed costs of buying or leasing premises in the financial trading model of your business plan. This way you can secure funding based on accepted parameters and then, when you find your premises, discuss any variations with the funder.

VARIABLES

There are a number of variables you will need to consider to define the premises for your business plan:

Location

Location should be based on the proximity to your marketplace as discussed in Chapter 2: Market research. You will have a clear idea of the ideal location for your nursery but bearing in mind the vagaries of premises acquisition, it will be sensible to have one or two alternative locations as well. Finding premises is time consuming and the broader your options regarding the area, the better the chances of early success.

Accessibility
Accessibility is a key issue. Regrettably, there is evidence to suggest that many parents select a nursery on the basis of its accessibility over its quality so whatever the location, make sure that customers can access it easily.

Buying or renting
Deciding whether to buy or lease premises may be determined by the source of your funding, the availability of premises in the area or your own long-term plans.

Size
The size of the building or the plot of land on which to build is likely to be determined by what you have identified as the number of childcare places needed by the market and your own philosophy regarding children's needs and ideal nursery size. From the perspective of profitability alone, economies of scale determine that larger nurseries tend to be more financially viable, as long as there is sufficient demand.

Type of building
There are three types of building from which to choose: newbuild, conversion or modular (see Chapter 8: Design.) The choices here may again be determined by the amount of funds you can raise. There are advantages and disadvantages with each (see table opposite).

Car parking
You may wish to discuss car parking with the highways section of your local planning department. Each area of the country has different views as to the parking and drop off requirements for a nursery.

Visibility
It is not essential that your nursery is in a clearly visible location such as on or very close to a main road or beside a school but it offers free marketing and in the right location can greatly improve the development rate of occupancy, or 'fill-rate'.

TYPES OF PREMISES: ADVANTAGES AND DISADVANTAGES

New build
Defined as constructing a nursery building on a plot.

Advantages

The design is to your own specification

It should be better operationally for staff and children (eg the nappy change will be near the baby room)

You can maximise the use of space more efficiently than in a conversion

It can be designed within a single storey

It can look clean, efficient and modern

Disadvantages

The costs are usually higher

It can take much longer to complete than other options

There will be a greater number of professionals involved

Conversion
Defined as converting an existing building into a nursery.

Advantages

It is quicker and less involved to arrange

The look is more traditional (if that is what you want)

In some conversions, it may often be possible to combine the benefits of a traditional frontage with the optimised layout of a purpose-built addition [1]

Disadvantages

The use of space is never ideal and you will need to consider the adaptability of the indoor areas

Amenities may be poorer (eg car parking and outdoor play space)

It may still take considerable time to arrange, particularly if a change of use is involved

Modular
Defined as putting a pre-designed and pre-fabricated building onto a plot and connecting it to services.

Advantages

It is much quicker and less involved to arrange than new build

It can be the least costly route

Disadvantages

The look of the building may not be as you would have designed it

The building will not last as long and may look worn earlier than the alternatives

Outdoor area

A well-planned outdoor area is essential to a nursery. In inner-cities a large outdoor play space may be hard to find. Whatever

---

[1] An excellent example of this is the Scuola dell'Infanzia e Asilo-nido, Cantalamessa, Bologna, Italy, which can be found on page 195 of *Kindergarten Architecture* by Mark Dudek, E&FN Spon (1996)

the situation, a brief discussion with the childcare registration officer will give you an idea of local authority requirements. An architect may help you be creative with a building or plot to give outdoor space where it may have been hard to achieve. Where outdoor play is limited, you may wish to consider the proximity of the nursery to alternative open space, such as local parks.

Storeys
Single storey premises on ground level are ideal but you may have to be prepared to accept two storey or more, depending upon your uses for the building.

Other amenities
Access to other amenities such as train stations, bus routes and shops may provide potential customers for you. Equally, good public transport to and from the nursery will help with the recruitment of staff.

Defined use
Each planning authority designates a use to a building

dependent upon its local plan. The use for nurseries is classed as D1 or D2 (in England and Wales; Class 10 in Scotland) and acquiring an existing building with this use will save time. Other buildings with the same defined use are schools and church premises.

PREMISES COSTS

Once you have created a specification for your nursery, you should call all the commercial estate agents operating in your selected locations to obtain details of land/property values or lease costs per square metre, so that you can build cost assumptions into your model.

The source of your funding will probably define what sort of premises you will ultimately operate in. If, for example, your funders prefer their investment to be asset-backed, you will be looking to acquire a site on which to build, or freehold premises to buy for conversion. Building or buying premises to convert are expensive options and it is perhaps more likely that you will only have the funds to take a lease on premises which you will need to convert. If so, it is reasonable to assume that you as tenant will have to bear the costs of conversion. Most nursery operators have found that few landlords have an understanding of the nursery market and are, therefore, unwilling to risk their own capital on converting their premises for a business sector they do not know.

SEARCHING FOR PREMISES

With your specification now clearly defined and your funding provisionally in place, you will be ready to begin the process of searching. There are a number of potential sources:

Estate agents
Contact all residential and commercial estate agents with your specification and keep in touch with them. They will be your best chance of finding suitable accommodation, and if you build up a good relationship with them, it will help your case.

Property developers

Property developers tend to be aware of plots of land or buildings which are not yet on the market (and may never come to the market). If they know of your plans to open a nursery and have your specifications, they may well be able to fit your nursery into a development scheme.

Residential builders/developers

On large-scale residential developments (of which there are many around the country), there is a requirement to provide infrastructure for the incoming residents, which tends to include a convenience store, post office, doctor's surgery and public house. These 'neighbourhood centres' can benefit from the addition of a day nursery. If you are looking for a site, many of the 'big name' residential developers may be prepared to let you have a small parcel of land on a development, or put you in touch with the partners responsible for the neighbourhood amenities in their development.

Local authority/planning department

Contact your local authority, it may have property of its own or be aware of property which would be suitable. The planning department will be able to tell you which properties are already designated for D1, D2 use.

Property press

Property trade magazines such as *Property Week* and *Estates Gazette* carry a myriad of properties for sale or rent, all over the UK. These publications are a good source of sites and buildings, but you will need to follow up each advertisement quickly as they are widely read.

Nursery agents

There is a small number of experienced nursery agents who handle the sale of existing nursery businesses in the UK (see Chapter 4: Buying a nursery). What is not widely known is that occasionally they have vacant premises for sale for use as a nursery and it may be worth your while registering your interest with them.

Local schools/education authorities

A large number of existing nurseries are located in the grounds of schools. Many local education authorities and independent schools are aware of a local need for childcare and can be sympathetic to a request for land, usually on a leased basis.

Look around

Make frequent trips to your desired location/s and keep an eye out for signboards offering lease or sale on premises or land. You can also make a note of empty buildings or plots and contact the local planning departments or the Land Registry to establish who the owner is and then make direct contact to see if they will consider a sale.

Architects

Architects have frequently assisted clients by bringing a site or building to their attention. If you have elected to use an architect (which is advisable and good value), it will be worth discussing your premises requirements in advance as they may be aware of something suitable.

Business development organisations

The Training Enterprise Council (Local Enterprise Council in Scotland) and Business Link are both bodies charged with supporting business development in their area and may be able to direct you towards suitable premises.

Network

Talk to everyone you are involved with, friends, business associates, bank manager, solicitor. Any of them may just lead you to the premises that becomes your new business address.

Summary

• *Prepare your specification based on the desired variables (that is lease or purchase, newbuild or conversion, desirable size, and so on)*

• *Contact local commercial agents and establish likely costs to put into your business plan*

• *Discuss your model with potential funders and agree parameters for the size and cost of the building*

• *Contact local commercial agents and other sources to instruct them to find sites/premises*

• *Be prepared to visit many sites before you find your ideal (and be ready to compromise, if necessary)*

• *Look for potential in each premises you see but be realistic about the conversion/building costs*

• *Involve a chartered surveyor and/or architect as early as you can*

PLANNING CONSENT

Whether you are buying land or a building, converting an existing building or erecting a modular construction, you will need to acquire planning consent. The local planners will take into account a number of issues including:

• *compliance with the unitary development plan (the local plan designating use for land buildings)*

- *compliance with any conservation criteria including listed buildings*

- *use and mixed use (you may wish to use some of the nursery as residential accommodation)*

- *external appearance and size*

- *traffic movements and parking*

- *noise or nuisance and residents' objections*

- *trees (especially those which are under Tree Preservation Order) and other environmental considerations*

It is, therefore, important not to commit to any acquisition before you have established its status with the planners and rendered your purchase/lease subject to a successful planning application. You will also want to speak to the childcare registration officer at the local authority at this point and if necessary ask for input on the design.

The planning consent process involves a formal application for which there will be a fee and you will need to submit detailed drawings of your proposed nursery, including any landscaping elements. Your architect will assist with this process.

Once the planning officer has conducted a full review of your application, s/he will then make a recommendation to the planning committee to approve or reject it. If the application is straightforward and carries the blessing of the planning officer's colleagues in other departments, such as highways, then the decision may be 'deferred' and simply granted by the officer, without referral to committee. If your application has to go to committee, it will wait until the monthly meeting following the review of the application. This process can take at least two months and considerably longer if there are issues to resolve.

It is essential, if you wish to avoid abortive planning application costs and architect's fees, that you sound out the planning officer as to what issues may be relevant, before submitting your application and ensure that your architect takes the officer's comments into account. You, or your architect, will need to follow the course of your application on its journey through the planning department to ensure that any concerns are dealt with and any necessary amendments made to your application. This may include liaising with other departments. If the officer recommends rejecting the application when it goes to committee, it is very unlikely that committee will overturn that recommendation.

Once approved, it is not uncommon for the planners to place restrictions on the use of the premises and, in the case of nurseries, they can occasionally limit the registered number of children based on their own requirements, rather than those of the authority responsible for registering the nursery. For example, a nursery may have space for 60 children but the planners may only allow the building to be used for 50 children if they believe that the traffic generated by parents' cars coming and going from a 60-place nursery would be excessive for its location. You might be able to appeal against such a restriction at a later date but success would not be guaranteed.

If you encounter problems with your application, you could involve a planning consultant. Throughout the country there are several planning consultants who have a rapport with the local planners and who are aware of their concerns and any likely restrictions. Some of the larger commercial estate agents that operate on a national basis also have a planning consultancy department. Fees can be high and results are not guaranteed but their expertise should not be underestimated and if it saves you starting the whole process again, from finding a site onwards, you may wish to seriously consider this option.

ACQUISITION

Once you have found suitable premises and are confident that planning consent will be granted, you may wish to run the process of acquisition in tandem with your planning application, to save time.

Freehold property

When buying an existing building freehold, you will need to retain the services of a solicitor to handle the transaction and it will be their role to establish clear 'title', that is that the premises are owned by the vendor and that it will be transferred to you unencumbered. The process is similar to buying a house and your solicitor will conduct searches and the appropriate stamp duty will be levied. You will also need a chartered surveyor to value the property which may, as in the case of house purchase, give you an opportunity to reduce the price. Before signing the contract to buy, make sure that everything, including planning consent, is in place.

Land

The process of buying land is very similar to that of acquiring freehold property but in addition you will want to be assured that the land is not contaminated in any way and that it will not present you with any unforeseen expense when you come to build on it. Your chartered surveyor will advise you about any tests that may need to be conducted on the land to ensure that it is fit for use. Land prices vary dramatically and it is not uncommon for two pieces of land of a similar size, in the same area to be priced very differently. So, take time to look around for the best deal. You will also want to be sure that you have taken into account the realistic costs of construction for your nursery before buying the land, so that you are able to operate within your budget.

Leasehold property

Most nurseries operate in leasehold premises, which means that the operator is a tenant in a building that they rent from a landlord. The terms of a lease can be very complex and are fraught with potential liabilities. Look closely at assignation,

OUTLINE PROCESS OF BUYING A SITE OR PROPERTY, ONCE LOCATED		Week 1	Week 2	Week 3	Week 4	Week 5	Week 6	Week 7	Week 8	Week 9	Week 10	Week 11	Week 12	Week 13	Week 14	Week 15	Week 16	Week 17	Week 18	Week 19	Week 20	Week 21	Week 22	Week 23	Week 24	Week 25	Week 26	Week 27	Week 28	Week 29	Week 30	Week 31	Week 32	Week 33	Week 34	Week 35	Week 36	Week 37	Week 38	Week 39	Week 40
Stage 1	Having located the site or property that best suits your needs, establish its feasibility by conducting a market appraisal of its potential.																																								
Stage 2	Decide whether to proceed with the acquisition of the site or property. The offer is then made and accepted subject to planning consent and satisfactory surveys.																																								
Stage 3	Contact the planners and brief an architect to produce preliminary drawings for planning purposes.																																								
Stage 4	Draw up the documentation necessary to secure funding, such as a full market report, showing likely number of customers and anticipated fee levels.																																								
Stage 5	The funding is agreed.																																								
Stage 6	Consult Social Services and make a full application to the planning authority with architect's drawings.																																								
Stage 7	The architect draws up a full specification for the site or property.																																								
Stage 8	The project manager/surveyor asks builders to tender against the full specification.																																								
Stage 9	Select builders from the tender process and award a contract. Planning is approved.																																								
Stage 10	The first site/premises meeting is held and the process of building/conversion begins.																																								
Stage 11	Construction/conversion process. This could take eight to 30 weeks depending on the project. Equipment is ordered.																																								
Stage 12	The interior of the nursery is fitted out and the equipment is delivered.																																								
Stage 13	The building is handed over and the equipment unpacked and set out.																																								
Stage 14	The appropriate officers issue certificates for fire, health and registration.																																								
Stage 15	The nursery opens. Any minor building works not completed are put right ('snagging' process).																																								

service charges, termination and the 'repairing' elements (that is repairs to the premises) of the lease and especially who, of landlord and tenant, is responsible for what. It is not within the scope of this book to go into detail concerning lease negotiation, suffice to say that without the benefit of good legal advice and the services of a competent chartered surveyor you could find yourself with onerous lease terms that could affect the profitability of your business.

Most leases have a built-in increase in rent after agreed periods. In the case of offices, the rents are set at market rent at the time. In the case of nurseries, there is no established norm on which to base an increase and many rents are based on the increase in the Retail Price Index (RPI) which is similar to the rate of inflation. It is reasonable to accept this principle when considering clauses covering rises in rent as it will, in effect, tie your rent increase to inflation.

On acquiring your premises, make sure that you immediately take out full insurance. You would be advised to discuss terms with a company which has nursery experience and a good insurance broker will be able to advise you.

RATES

Your nursery will attract rates, payable to the Council on an ongoing basis and you will need to budget for these in your financial model. Your premises will have a rateable value and you will then pay a level of pence in the pound each year.

Many nurseries are operating in premises where the rate assessment is too high and you can appeal against this after acquisition. There are a number of professional agencies which deal with appeals and claim their fees as a percentage of money saved. It may be worth contacting them to look at your case and establish if there is a saving to be made.

8: DESIGN

WHATEVER NURSERY ENVIRONMENT you choose to provide, it will affect the children in it. There is evidence to show that too little space causes bullying, and a poorly-lit space makes children listless, whereas a well-designed, stimulating environment can produce lively and contented children.

THE IMPORTANCE OF DESIGN

Architect and author of *Kindergarten Architecture* Mark Dudek believes that the design of a nursery is fundamental to the children's well-being: 'The value of good design for pre-school children and their carers is related primarily to the potential for a nursery to provide an environment within which children can develop social skills and sensibilities through interaction with their peers and adult carers.'[1] If the building is inappropriate then this socialising process will not take place.

Practicalities
The three options in nursery construction are: purpose-build, conversion (with or without an element of new build) and a pre-fabricated/modular construction.

Whichever route you choose, you will need to consider the design elements. If you elect to use one of the many pre-fabricated nursery companies, you may not need the services of an architect, but the project will still need to be managed by a surveyor or someone with similar project management experience.

There are a number modular building suppliers such as Terrapin, Speaks, Global Mobile, Tingdene, Portakabin, all of

[1] 'Space matters', *Starting a Nursery, Nursery World (Summer 1998), p22*

which have experience in the nursery sector. Try and see one or two modular buildings that have been operational for a few years to get a good idea of their quality. Portakabin linked up with Cottrell & Vermuelen, one of the more exciting architectural practices in the UK with experience of nursery design, to produce an interesting new modular nursery called Lilliput, which is worth consideration.

UP FOR DISCUSSION

If you opt for purpose-built or converted premises, then discuss the following key elements with your architect:

- allocation of indoor space to room size and function
- allocation of space per child, by age
- private places (pre-school children are attracted to small spaces, so providing areas where children can remain relatively undisturbed may be worth consideration)
- function of the outdoor space/s
- layout of rooms in relation to each other so that amenities can be accessed easily
- colour and decor
- natural light and lighting
- heating and the effect of seasonal temperature variation
- extraction/ventilation
- wall and floor coverings
- materials and textures
- sound
- hygiene, safety and security
- regulations
- soft furnishings
- costs
- your curriculum decisions, your personal philosophy and market research findings and how this will impact on the nursery design
- design constraints of the building

Space requirements

Much of what is broadly expected of a modern nursery is laid down in the Children Act 1989. Local guidelines based on the Children Act can be obtained from the registration authority, within the local authority, and will detail the space requirements for each child. These guidelines are also likely to affect other aspects of nursery design, and you should incorporate recommendations from the environmental health department and fire officer into the project. Many design issues are covered in *Starting and Running a Nursery*, which is worth referring to on this subject[2].

DESIGN ELEMENTS

In your design, you will need to include most of the facilities listed (in alphabetical order) below:

Interior

Activity space

Some nurseries provide a room for each age group of children in which the group conducts all its activities (sleeping, eating, playing and so on) and have no shared activity rooms. It is important to try to include at least one large communal area, which can be used by different age groups for a wide range of activities, particularly those activities which require space, such as drama, dance and music and movement.

Child rooms

Baby Rooms: Each baby requires 3.72 m^2 clear space (that is net of any built-in storage). If possible, it is advisable to allow an extra 20 per cent to ensure that you comply with your local guidelines. Further facilities should include direct access to a well-ventilated nappy changing area, a milk kitchen, washing and wet play facilities and access to a toilet.

Toddler Rooms: Each toddler requires 2.79m^2 and again it is advisable to provide an extra 20 per cent. Other facilities should include direct access to nappy changing area, toilets, washing and wet play. Toys, books and equipment should be stored at child height.

[2] H. Jameson and M. Watson *Starting and Running a Nursery* Stanley Thornes (1998), p68

Pre-school rooms: Each pre-school child requires 2.32 m^2 and it is advisable to provide an additional 10 to 15 per cent. In addition, you should seek access to toilets, an art and craft area, built in storage and washing and wet play facilities.

It is important to bear in mind that the children will need room to rest or sleep. You should, therefore, create an area within or separate to these child rooms for this purpose.

Circulation space

Try to ensure that all circulation space, such as corridors, do not impinge upon the children's rooms as it can be very disrupting for children if rooms are used as a corridor.

Coats and hats

Pegs for coats and hats should be labelled for each child and at child height to encourage independence.

Kitchen

Ideally, there should be additional external access to the kitchen for deliveries, and it is preferable if the kitchen is of a commercial standard and includes stainless steel equipment. You will need to comply with all relevant health and safety regulations. Generous amounts of food storage space and a servery are an advantage.

Laundry

The laundry should be separate and include a washer and drier along with worktops and shelving. It will be in frequent use for bedding and may also be used for children's clothing and staff uniforms.

Milk kitchen

Milk kitchen/s should be as near as possible to the baby areas and include a small fridge, sink and noticeboards to specify important information such as formula preferences, feed times and dietary needs.

Office

There should be an administration office for the manager/officer in charge. Ideally, it should have a view of the main entrance to the nursery so that s/he is aware people entering and leaving the building.

Pram and buggy store

To keep the nursery tidy and as a service to parents, it is useful to have a dry pram and buggy store easily accessible to the main entrance.

Reception area

This is the area where parents and children are welcomed to the nursery and should include seating and information.

Staff room

This should include a small kitchen area for tea making facilities, safe storage for clothes and valuables, easy chairs and noticeboards. Encourage staff to make it as homely as they wish.

Storage

There is a great need for storage space in all the child rooms and throughout the nursery. Try to include as much accessible storage space as possible.

Toilets

There is usually a minimum requirement of one WC to every ten children. You will also need the same number of wash handbasins. A disabled toilet and staff/visitor's toilets will also be required.

Training room and library

If you plan to include staff training in your nursery then a dedicated training room, where reference books can be kept, will be a boon. It will allow you to carry out your training plans without disturbance and encourage the sense that training is valued.

Interior/exterior

Open activity space

For hot summer days and for fresh air in winter, it is advisable to create an area which can be opened to the air but which remains covered to give access to fresh air and protection from the elements.

Exterior

Car parking

It is likely that you will be required to provide a certain number of car parking spaces for parents to drop off their children and for staff.

Kitchen bin area

A discreet bin area should be made available next to the kitchen for kitchen waste.

Outdoor play areas

A safe outdoor play area with fencing of at least 1.6m high is essential. Ideally, this will be divided into a number of areas offering different uses, for example, hard surface for all-weather use, grass, wet-pour (springy tarmac) and play-bark.

If possible, make a transition area from the garden to the nursery where children can wipe any mud and water from their feet.

Select outdoor play equipment – fixed or movable – with care. A range of different providers of such equipment can be found in *Nursery World*, its supplement *Nursery Equipment* and other trade press.

Consider providing a quiet area for sleeping babies close to the baby room where prams and buggies can be put under cover or in shade.

Outdoor storage will be required for trikes and other equipment.

Retain or add trees and other forms of shading wherever possible (willow is fast growing), and take care to eliminate poisonous or otherwise dangerous plants, shrubs and trees, in particular foxglove, laburnum and yew and thorned or spiked varieties.

It is unlikely that you will be able to obtain actual designs for good nurseries but you would do well to buy a copy of Mark Dudek's *Kindergarten Architecture*, which includes 21 interesting designs from around the world and which are sure to inspire you. All are worthy of close investigation and in particular the Stensby Personalbarnehage, Akerhus, a 60-place nursery in Norway, detailed in the book.[3]

[3] M. Dudek, *Kindergarten Architecture* E&FN Spon (1996), p174

9: REGULATION AND INSPECTION

THERE IS A MAZE **of regulation surrounding nursery operation, which you must navigate effectively if your business is to succeed (see box page 85). You will need to consider such issues as your responsibilities as an employer, setting up the premises and crucially, registration.**

BECOMING A CARING EMPLOYER

There is complex legislation designed to protect the rights of employees, however if you aim to be a 'caring employer' you should, in essence, uphold your responsibilities. So what defines a caring employer?

As a minimum your duties will include:

• *behaving reasonably in matters of employment*

• *practising good industrial relations such as clear disciplinary and grievance procedures*

• *taking reasonable care to ensure the safety and health of your employees*

• *paying your employees when you have agreed to do so*

You will need to be aware of your legal responsibilities and obligations and the Arbitration Conciliation & Advisory Service (ACAS) produce useful guides. In brief, key employers' obligations include:

• *operating a PAYE system – deducting tax and employer's and employee's National Insurance contributions*

• *providing a written health and safety policy*

• *operating a Statutory Sick Pay (SSP) scheme (after four days' sick leave, employees are entitled to a minimum statutory payment)*

• *operating a Statutory Maternity Pay (SMP) scheme*

Details regarding employers' full responsibilities can also be obtained from your local Social Security office. You will need to be careful when recruiting to ensure that you comply with race, sex and disability discrimination law. In addition, all employees are legally required to have a contract of employment two months after starting work which specifies date of employment, job title, remuneration, hours and entitlements.

If you have concerns, the Institute of Personnel and Development (IPD) have a legal advice line but you need to have membership to access it. So a good source of advice might be an IPD member, if you happen to know one. In general, try to make sure you have access to good advice for times when you may need it.

REGISTRATION

Once the premises are ready, as a daycare provider you have a legal obligation to register with the local authority in order to operate. This means that you need to be familiar with the relevant section of the Children Act 1989 applying to premises. This can be obtained from The Stationery Office and you will need to request: The Children Act 1989 Guidance & Regulations, Volume 2, Family Support, Day Care and Educational Provision for Young Children.

At present, each local authority applies its own interpretation of the Children Act[1]. It will be necessary for you to request a copy of these interpretations called the "local guidelines" from your authority and, in some areas, a charge is made. There will also be a charge of £110 when you come to make your full application.

The rules and regulations are far reaching and cover staffing ratios, child space requirements, records, resources, premises and the 'fitness'[2] of you and your staff to run a nursery. Falling foul of the rules can be disastrous and the onus is on you to ensure constant compliance. However, when you consider that there are some 7,000 registered private day nurseries operating in the UK at present, compliance is not an insurmountable problem.

The registration officer within your local authority is there to help and will welcome discussion at an early stage. You might wish to begin the liaison when you start designing the nursery and build up an early rapport. The relationship needs to be based on trust and your registration officer will want to be assured that you have considered the children's needs.

There is no short cut to reading through the Children Act and the local guidelines. It is important to say that many authorities apply different interpretations of the Act and some of the local guidelines are based on their own experience and philosophy. It is not unusual, for example, that a registration authority will seek different staff-to-child ratios for babies than the Children Act specifies. These are invariably higher ratios than the Act and will involve you employing more staff than ordinarily required, which will have an effect on the profitability of your business. It

---

[1] On 2 August 1999 government minister Margaret Hodge announced a range of changes to the system of regulation including: 'One consistent and uniform set of standards for all providers.' A new arm of Ofsted will be set up and given responsibility for inspecting all care and education aspects of day nurseries. Changes are likely to be implemented over the next two years and in the meantime the current situation will prevail

[2] The manager/officer in charge needs to considered 'fit' for the task of running a nursery as defined by the Children Act. This means holding a relevant qualification in childcare, early years education, social work, health visiting, or children's nursing and having experience of working with young children

is therefore vital that you acquire the guidelines covering the area in which you are going to operate before making financial projections.

If your philosophy is at variance with your local authority guidelines, you would be advised to discuss this with them to establish what compromises may be achieved. You can follow an appeal procedure if you consider a decision to be inappropriate, but you should seek to ensure that at all times the relationship remains one of mutual respect between operator and registration authority.

Your registration officer will visit at least once a year and advise you in advance each time. They will conduct an inspection and provide you with a report which may contain points to be actioned by you. These points may cover anything in their scope of reference from replacing a stair gate to improving children's access to books. If you disagree with any of their observations or action points, you should be given an opportunity to air your views and, if agreed, have your inspection report amended accordingly before the final draft.

Between visits, you will need to bear in mind that it is your responsibility to communicate any changes within the nursery which the registration authority considers important.

There is also a compliance procedure for staff. This involves a police check which can take considerable time and, in the case of new employees, delays can leave you temporarily understaffed. It is therefore important to gain agreement in advance with your registration officer that you are able to conditionally employ staff in the nursery, before finalising the necessary checks. Many registration officers will accept this principle but they are likely to impose conditions; for example a member of staff awaiting a police check may only work on a supervised basis until receiving clearance.

Many of the key requirements of the Children Act are outlined in the box below:

NURSERY REGISTRATION REQUIREMENTS

Premises

Children Act 1989 requirements relating to premises cover:

- access to a safe garden or outside play area

- hygienic washing and toilet facilities

- hygienic food preparation

- the safety of the kitchen

- quality, quantity and range of equipment and materials

- space per child: 0-2s require $3.7m^2$; 2-3s require $2.8\ m^2$; 3-5s require $2.3m^2$. (Note that these space requirements can vary locally)

- furniture and toys, which must be both sufficient and safe

- play material, which have to reflect a range of cultural, religious and linguistic backgrounds

Staff

- The officer in charge and deputy need to be qualified in childcare, early years education, social work, health visiting or children's nursing

- Officers in charge are supernumerary if there are more than 20 children attending

- All staff need to be 'fit' to work with children and need to be to have undergone a police check

- Adult:child ratios depend on children's ages: 0-2s ratio 1:3; 2-3 ratio 1:4; 3-5 ratio 1:8. (Note that these can vary locally)

- Additional staff ratios may be required for children with special needs

- At least half the staff should be appropriately qualified and others should follow appropriate training

- References should be taken up

- Staff should be aware of health and safety requirements

- There should be suitably trained first aiders

Recording procedures

Nursery records should include:

- details of all children and staff

- a daily register

- accident records

- information for parents

- medicine records

- insurance records

- child protection policy

- behaviour and sanctions policy

- a written health and safety policy

- a written assessment of the risks to staff and children

- You should also carry out regular health inspections and audits

SUMMARY OF RELEVANT LEGISLATION AND GUIDELINES		
Responsibilities	**References**	**Legislation**

Employers'
– *Terms of*
  employment
		– *Employment Protection*
		  (Consolidation) Act 1978
		– *Trade Union Reform and*
		  Employment Rights Act
		  1993

– *Advertising/*
  recruiting
		– *Sex Discrimination Act*
		  1975
		– *Race Relations Act 1976*
		– *Disability Discrimination*
		  Act

– *Pay*		– *Equal Pay Act 1970*
– *'Fitness' for* *childcare work*	– *Local police checks*	

Premises
– *Set-up*
	– *Local planning authority*
	
	– *Under-eights registration*
	  officer
	
	– *Fire officer*
	
	– *Environmental health*
	  officer
		– *Unitary development*
		  plan
		– *Local authority*
		  guidelines from the
		  Registration and
		  Inspection Unit
		– *The Fire Precautions Act*
		  1971
		– *Health and Safety at*
		  Work Act 1974
		– *Management of Health*
		  and Safety at Work
		  Regulations 1992
		– *Health and Safety (First*
		  Aid) Regulations 1982
		– *The Reporting of Injuries,*
		  Death and Diseases and
		  Dangerous Occurrences
		  Regulations 1981
		– *The Electricity at Work*
		  Act 1989
		– *The Food Safety Act 1990*

Registration	– *Under-eights registration*
	  officer
		– *Children Act 1989*
		  Guidance and
		  Regulations Volume 2
		– *Local authority*
		  guidelines from the
		  Registration and
		  Inspection Unit

10: MARKETING AND CUSTOMER CARE

THERE ARE MANY PEOPLE OUT THERE looking for good childcare and willing to pay. You, hopefully, will soon be there providing a quality service. Parents may have searched in vain for good childcare and you could potentially search in vain for customers. The magic required to bring you both together is 'marketing'.

WHAT IS MARKETING?

Marketing is simply finding out what the customer needs and providing it. In the childcare sector, there are many customers with an immediate childcare need and demand is currently greater than supply. However, you will still need to create and maintain awareness, establish the optimum price, deliver quality and nurture your clients if you are to succeed. To ensure that you do that efficiently will require planning. It will also need considerable effort and many people underestimate the time it takes to market their business effectively.

The time to begin is when you know that you have secured your premises and set an approximate opening date. Ideally, you should have about six months in which to conduct your pre-opening marketing but this often coincides with the premises being converted, so let us assume that you have two to three months. During this time you should be marketing in earnest to ensure that you open your nursery with as many children as is operationally feasible on day one.

Marketing methods

You can attract business to your nursery in various ways:

- *signage*
- *advertising*
- *PR*
- *leafleting/postering*
- *sales*
- *open days/exhibitions*
- *other methods, such as billboards and blimps*

Marketing channels

Before you start, you will need to do a little more research. Not market research, although the information you gleaned from that process will be useful, but 'marketing research'. Marketing research is the process of establishing where you are going to advertise, where you will place your signage or send your press releases and how you are going to distribute your leaflets and so on. You will have a range of channels through which you can market your nursery:

- *local newspapers and magazines*

- *Yellow Pages/Thomson Local*

- *local TV and radio*

- *community locations, such as libraries, health centres, hospitals and shops*

- *local employer channels, such as in-house magazines, noticeboards and e-mail*

- *signage locations*

- *social services*

The table below shows which methods you might use for which channels:

Channels	Methods
Local newspapers and magazines	*Advertising and PR*
Yellow Pages/ Thomson Local	*Advertising*
Local TV and radio	*PR (and possibly some radio advertising)*
Community locations	*Posters, leaflets, advertising, exhibition stands*
Local employer channels	*PR, sales, exhibition stands*
Signage locations	*Permanent signage and banners*
Social Services	*Make sure you are included in their local nursery list*

Checklist

To ensure that you can select the best channels to publicise your nursery location you will need to source all the appropriate information first. Use the following marketing research checklist:

• *Send for media packs from local newspapers, magazines and directories (such as Yellow Pages). These tell you when the publications appear, their distribution/circulation, their rates, their advertising contact names and any special features which may be of interest. You will also need the editors' names so that you can invite them to any newsworthy function or event*

• *Find out the contacts for local radio (and possibly TV if you are doing something particularly newsworthy) so that you can get news releases to their newsdesk*

• *Contact the local hospital, library, and any other public meeting place to see if you can display posters and leave leaflets and find out if there will be any charge*

• *Establish a good location for your signs and banners and if necessary obtain planning consent first from your local planning officer*

• *Find out all the names and contacts in local companies so that you can approach them to publicise your nursery through them*

• *Establish the costs of design and production of marketing materials, especially if you are having them designed by a graphic design/marketing agency (see Marketing materials below)*

Marketing spend

Once you have obtained the information you need, you can then begin to plan your marketing spend. The key to effective marketing is targeting. The better you 'target' your marketing, the harder your marketing spend will be working for you. For example, if you are placing an advertisement for your nursery in a local newspaper it is likely to be more effective in the women's pages than in the motoring section.

The charts below, Cost per enquiry and Percentage of enquiries, show an analysis of enquiries for a typical nursery. Advertising and signage are the most effective but all methods are worth pursuing to see if one is more effective than another in

Cost per enquiry

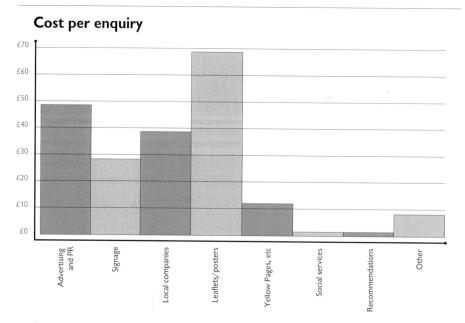

Percentage of enquiries

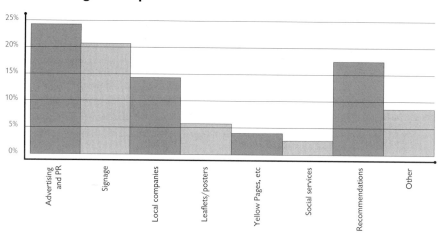

your location. If you monitor where all your enquiries come from, you will quickly learn which are the most cost-effective methods for your nursery.

MARKETING PLAN

Once you have established some costs and decided upon the methods you want to use, you will be ready to prepare your plan, which will be in two main parts: Marketing materials and the Implementation plan.

Marketing materials

Marketing materials are the leaflets, posters and other materials that you will need to access the marketing channels you have selected. The essentials are as follows:

Marketing materials	Needs to include	Notes
Signage or posters to attract enquiries.	*Name and Location of nursery • Contacts • Hours of opening*	*Make them as big and as bold as possible and provide only essential information.*
Leaflets for publicity purposes (flyers) to attract enquiries.	*Name and location of nursery • Childcare service (age of children, times of opening, etc) • Contacts*	*Keep the design simple, and if possible, include a map*
Advertisements to attract enquiries	*Name and location of nursery • Childcare service • Contacts • Any selling points (eg swimming pool or dance and drama)*	*The bigger and simpler in design, the better. Ask for them to appear on right hand pages near the front of the publication*
Brochure or information sheet to respond to enquiries	*Name and location of nursery • Prices • Details of childcare service • Curriculum • Facilities/equipment • Philosophy • Booking procedure • Special needs • Parent/nursery partnership • Contacts • Menu • Staff and training information*	*Keep the design simple and remember that a picture tells a thousand words.*
Registration folder for bookings	*Settling in procedure • Registration documents (parent information required by nursery) • Parent/nursery agreement • Fee details • Contacts*	*Provide only essential information*

You may also wish to consider other materials such as the child development records that you produce for parents, newsletters, policies that are displayed for parents, and information for companies where you could publicise your service to employees.

When you have decided on the materials to use, you can cost the design and production. To begin, it is worth investing in a distinctive logo for your company that spells quality. Try and find a balance between the production of your materials and the distribution of them so that you communicate a quality image to your potential customers, while distributing the information as widely as possible to your target audience. You will want to develop a 'house style' so that whatever appears from your company is consistent with other materials that you produce.

Implementation plan

Bearing in mind the fact that you will be marketing your nursery before it opens, a typical implementation, with estimated costs, could be drawn up as follows:

Pre-opening

• *Erect a banner/sign on (or near) the site at the earliest opportunity. Cost: £500*

• *Compile a press pack for the local press. Seek a photo opportunity with the target press as soon as the sign is fitted. Otherwise commission a photographer and distribute the photos with the press pack. Cost: £100*

• *Request company information from local Chambers of Commerce and mailshot local companies. Cost: £200 for company information and mailshot*

• *Prepare advertisements in the 'house style' for pre-opening advertising in selected local press and other media. Cost: £300 for each advertisement placed*

• *Prepare information leaflets (including map) for household distribution. Arrange for local newsagents to distribute leaflets. Cost: £200 for leaflet distribution*

• *Contact local hospitals as poster sites. Cost: £50 each*

• *Contact Yellows Pages and/or Thomson Local about the deadline for directory advertising and prepare and place an advertisement. Cost: £500 for each placement*

• *Fit a permanent sign. Cost: £700*

Opening ceremony

• *Identify and invite local companies to attend the opening ceremony. Plan catering for the day. Cost: £300 for buffet and drinks*

• *Invite the local press to attend. Have press packs available on the day*

• *Invite a celebrity or your local MP to perform the opening ceremony*

Post opening

• *Advertise an open week for all potential customers. Invite key*

influence groups such as local schools, health visitors and representatives of the local National Childbirth Trust, social services and Chambers of Commerce

- *Continue advertising, PR and sales on a budgeted basis*

The table opposite shows a sample marketing budget for a fictitious nursery in its first year.

GREENHOUSE NURSERY MARKETING BUDGET

BUDGET YEAR 1	Signage	Press advertising	Other advertising	Directory ads	PR/ Photography	Leaflet drops	Company mailshot	Corporate information	Official opening	TOTAL
Month 1	500				100			100		700
Month 2						300				300
Month 3		300				200	100			600
Month 4										
Month 5		300								300
Month 6	700			500	500					1,700
Month 7 (opening)		300	200						300	800
Month 8										
Month 9		300								300
Month 10										
Month 11		300								300
Month 12										
TOTAL	1,200	1,500	200	500	600	500	100	100	300	5,000

OCCUPANCY DEVELOPMENT

Once your nursery begins to fill, you will want to ensure that you can meet demand by 'creating' places in your nursery. The more flexible your nursery, the better occupancy you are liable to achieve. This may mean no longer thinking in terms of age groups and rooms, such as a '12-18 month Toddler Room' for example, but thinking of your nursery as a child space and how best to meet demand, and the needs of the children, in that space.

Try as well to anticipate the peaks and troughs in occupancy. Every year many nurseries lose a large number of children to school around August. You should be able to avoid a downturn in occupancy figures by establishing the number of leavers well in advance. Marketing to increase demand and acquire children will then replace those leavers.

Fees

The price you charge will make a considerable difference to the speed of your occupancy development – that is, how quickly the nursery fills. You may, therefore, wish to open with a low price to fill quickly and then charge more once you are covering your costs. However, it is hard to increase the fee level to existing customers, so you may wish to hold out for a higher fee and take longer to fill the nursery. It is up to you to find the balance which delivers the optimum result but remember that it is better to be trading than waiting for customers.

To establish an acceptable opening fee level, you can gauge the fee levels of the competition (see Chapter 2: Market research). This method is important but you must also ensure that you charge a fee level appropriate to your costs and which is sustainable by the market. Once your costs are covered, your price can be more market driven. This means that the greater the demand, the higher the potential price. For example, if there are ten parents chasing one baby place, the price can go up. Of course the converse is true, if there are ten baby places chasing one parent, the price will have to come down.

CUSTOMER CARE

You will have two sets of customers – 'internal' and 'external'. The internal customers are your staff and the external customers are the parents paying for childcare. You will need to look after both.

Staff
Customer care involves caring for your staff. Rather than training them to perform a range of set customer-care tasks, which may be limited in scope and short-lived, true customer care derives from a member of staff feeling valued and thus valuing others. So, your customer care plan will need to include your internal customers as well as external. In their role caring for external customers, your staff will need to be aware of the needs of parents and their own role in ensuring their continued satisfaction.

Parents
In relation to your external customers, the parents, customer care is simply ongoing marketing – continuing the process of market research and satisfying needs. Once you are trading, you will want to ensure that the needs of the customers you already have are met in the best possible way and the easiest way to get that right is to listen.

Listening to your customers means providing them with as many opportunities to communicate with you as possible. In particular, you will want to organise regular parents' meetings so that parents have the opportunity to raise issues of concern with you. You can then respond comprehensively to their concerns, so that the nursery operates in partnership with them, meeting their needs, while you remain in control.

As a suggestion, conduct parents' meetings once a quarter, keep them on an informal basis and include staff. You may also wish to encourage parents to appoint their own representatives. Their role would be to represent the views of absent parents at the meeting and to report back to those absentees. Continue to hold meetings even if you have poor attendance. Once you have heard parents' views, you will need to respond to their needs or offer a well-reasoned explanation as to why you are unable to do so. Difficulties may arise when parents have conflicting expectations but you will need to steer a steady course between their demands, always remembering that they may not have your (and your team's) level of understanding of what is best in the nursery setting.

You will also need to provide your customers with as much information as possible. One of the most common complaints from parents is that they were not told ('I didn't know that there was a case of chicken pox in the nursery. Why wasn't I told?', 'I didn't know that sand and water play was the basis for early maths. Why didn't you tell me?')

Take every opportunity using signs, noticeboards, letters, newsletters, memos and meetings to provide parents with the information you think they will need and then ask them if they are happy with the amount of information they receive.

One of the best ways to solicit information from parents is through a questionnaire. You can compile a questionnaire on any topic on which you wish to solicit their opinion or views. The sample opposite covers booking a place in the nursery:

GREENHOUSE NURSERY CUSTOMER SATISFACTION QUESTIONNAIRE

So that we can ensure that our service meets your needs, we would be grateful if you could take a moment to complete the questionnaire below:

When you enquired about a place at the nursery:	Yes	No	Comments
did we respond courteously and send our information quickly enough?			
was the information that we sent useful?			
If you decided not to visit the nursery, could you explain why?			
When you visited the nursery:	Yes	No	Comments
what were your first impressions?			
was the manager courteous and helpful?			
did the staff work well with the children?			
were the children's activities explained to you?			
were you and your child made to feel welcome?			

When you enquired about a place at the nursery:	Yes	No	Comments
were we able to accommodate any specific needs you requested for your child?			
was the nursery clean?			
If you decided not to book a place at the nursery, could you explain why?			
When you booked a place at the nursery:	Yes	No	Comments
did the manager/officer in charge handle your booking efficiently?			
was the booking information clear?			
did the manager/officer in charge explain the procedure clearly (eg settling in your child or payment details)			

Thank you for your time in completing the questionnaire

11: MANAGEMENT AND STAFFING

THE BUSINESS OF CHILDCARE **is oriented around people and while the people business is hard work, it can also be very rewarding.**

Any business which employs lots of people has both a duty and a responsibility to understand how to get the best out of them. This involves taking steps to ensure they are happy in the workplace and doing jobs for which they are suited. There is also a collective responsibility shared by the team – that no one lets the side down – and it will be your role to monitor that.

If one of the motivating factors in starting your own business is to exercise power, then you may try to control employees in a way which is counter-productive to their performance. Your power may be a negative influence on the business. Managing people properly will require you to play the role of facilitator and it is this responsibility which generates the volume of work.

People in the workplace are primarily motivated by being respected, valued and above all listened to. They also like to be given the opportunity to extend themselves within a framework of security. You will need to take time to engender a culture of this in staff who have responsibility for others, such as managers, deputies or room leaders. And, if you make the effort to put this framework in place, it brings its own practical rewards – low staff turnover (essential in the nursery business) and high staff morale. This in turn results in a positive, fulfilled team delivering good interactive practice between carer and

child. Staff satisfaction goes a long way to defining the quality of your business and making a happy, successful nursery.

The converse also applies. Any attempt to skimp on the work involved in good management will mean that you will endlessly be chasing the tail of problems associated with high staff turnover and low morale. As touched on in Chapter 4: Buying a nursery, breaking the habits of bad practice in a nursery, at a time when concerned parents may be removing their children, requires far greater effort than the work involved in setting up good practice in the first place.

Assuming your own background is as an early years professional, you will understand the needs of children and how best to develop them and facilitate learning experiences for them. As an employer in a childcare setting, you will need to understand and meet the needs of your staff and create developmental opportunities for them. Ideally, this will involve formal training for your staff, and for you.

MANAGEMENT TRAINING

In recognition of how vital it is to a business, the shelves of the management section of any bookshop are stacked with training information. And if you acknowledge the benefits of any training that you have received, you will understand the gains that you and your senior staff can receive from formal training.

It is not within the scope of this book to provide a substitute for leadership training. There are many organisations providing such training and your local Training Enterprise Council (Local Enterprise Council in Scotland) or Chambers of Commerce will provide information about them. Alternatively, the trade magazines for human resources managers provide copious information about training[1].

There are many important skills that can be learned through formal training:

• *You will understand more clearly the role that you naturally tend to play as part of a team and the roles others play and how to use these to the benefit of the team*[2]

• *You will see that not everyone learns in the same way and that people need to be able to learn in a way that is most appropriate to their style*

• *You will establish that there are various management styles you can use and that these have to be used appropriately, that is on the right occasion with the right person in order to achieve the best results*

• *You will see that people are motivated by a range of 'satisfiers' and 'dissatisfiers' – things that people consider important in their work. One of the most significant of these is achievement*

• *You will learn how to employ people who have complementary skills to yours to make the team operate more efficiently*

These are not just tricks of the management trade but are genuine insights into human behaviour which can help your business succeed.

---

[1] For example, *Management Today, Personnel Today, Human Resources,* which are readily available on the newstands

[2] These are known as Belbin's Team Roles developed by occupational psychologist J Meredith Belbin

NURSERY MANAGER'S ROLE

Whether you intend to manage the nursery yourself or employ a manager to run it, whenever you are not there the business will be reliant upon the skills of your understudy. So, whoever you delegate that responsibility to will need to have the skills required. Understanding the role of manager will help, and it is a vital role. A nursery manager has wide-ranging responsibilities, representing diverse and occasionally conflicting interests, including the interests of:

- *the children*
- *the staff*
- *the parents*
- *the management/nursery owner*
- *any company involved in the nursery (if they are sponsoring places)*
- *the local community*

This juggling act involve managers in performing a number of roles including:

* *staff managers – they need to understand how to manage, motivate and discipline staff*

* *trainers – they need to be able to pass on their skills and knowledge and ensure that others do so*

* *childcarers – they obviously need to be a 'fit' person as defined by the Children Act but depending on the size and staffing structure of the nursery they may also be involved in hands-on childcare*

* *facilities managers – they have to be able to deal with the little problems that can occur in running a premises, such as washing machines breaking down and power failures, while still keeping an eye on the important issues of health and safety in the workplace*

* *budget holders – they may need to be able to manage expenditure and income and account for both in a precise and intelligible way*

* *PR and sales people – they always represent you and your organisation, especially at the point of sale when showing people around the nursery*

* *customer carers – they need to use all the skills of diplomacy at their disposal in dealing with parents and their concerns*

* *negotiators – they have to negotiate to ensure that the needs of all the interest groups are represented and that the reasonable demands of any one group are adequately met or that any disputes are effectively resolved*

STAFFING STRUCTURE

Depending on your premises and any plans you may have for training, you will want to put in place a structure to define which staff you require and at which level.

Below is a sample staff structure for a medium-sized (56-place) nursery operating at capacity. It includes a number of trainee staff and has assumed that the child/age breakdown is as follows:

Age	Actual child numbers	Assumed number of rooms	Minimum staff requirement (based on Children Act guidelines) not including supernumerary staff
0–24 mths	24	3	8
24–36 mths	16	2	4
36+ mths	16	1	2
Total	**56**		**14**

SUGGESTED STAFFING STRUCTURE FOR A 56-PLACE NURSERY			
Room	**Registered child numbers**	**Primary role**	**Additional role**
Baby room 1	9	Room leader Qualified staff Unqualified staff	Trainer/mentor Mentor Trainee
Baby room 2	9	Room leader Qualified staff Unqualified staff	Trainer/mentor Mentor Trainee
Baby room 3	6	Room leader Qualified staff	Trainer/mentor Mentor
Toddler room 1	8	Room leader Qualified staff Unqualified staff	Trainer/mentor Mentor Trainee and shared assistant with other rooms
Toddler room 2	8	Room leader Qualified staff	Trainer/mentor Mentor
Pre-school room	16	Room leader Qualified staff Unqualified staff	Trainer/mentor/teacher Mentor Trainee and shared assistant with other rooms
Total staff		16	
Minimum staff required by Children Act guidelines		14	

'Overstaffing'

The suggested staffing structure (see table opposite) allows for more staff than is required under the Children Act, and despite the additional cost, there are major benefits to 'overstaffing' in such a way.

Many nurseries spend more money on agency fees to cover staff holidays and illness than they would on permanently employing additional staff. Time is saved by having the additional staff in situ, instead of chasing relief or agency staff. The nursery benefits from improved continuity of care and you avoid having to bring in agency staff who do not know the children, are unfamiliar with the staff team or your policies and procedures and are not known to the parents.

If you have qualified assessors and mentors as members of your senior staff, then you can reap the benefits of training staff in NVQ II and III in Childcare and Education on the premises. Firstly, you may be able to take on a training contract from your local Training and Enterprise Council (Local Enterprise Council in Scotland) and receive training payments for each trainee. You will also engender in the senior staff a sense of pride in their work if they feel they are setting an example for the less experienced members of staff.

Regrettably, in childcare there is a high turnover of nursery staff. This is not unusual in a sector where salaries are low and the workforce is predominantly young women. You will probably find that even if you staff your nursery above the requirements, it will still be essential to have a good bank of relief staff – temporary staff, who can come in at short notice and are already part of the team. And you may still need to consider a relationship with a local friendly nursery-staffing agency.

You may also wish to use part-time staff so that there is an element of job sharing among the team. This arrangement can help when it comes to holiday and illness cover because only half the time needs to be covered and the part-time staff member may be able to increase their hours temporarily to assist. However, it is preferable to maintain as much continuity in the baby rooms, including having consistency throughout the day, so perhaps seek part-time carers for the older children only.

STAFF RECRUITMENT

As new nurseries continue to open throughout the UK, there is a shortage of qualified staff. In some areas, particularly around London and the Southeast of England, this shortage is acute.

When operating in a competitive market for staff, any 'edge' over your competitors will give you an advantage. If you apply marketing techniques to the recruitment process, you can improve your chances of taking on quality staff. This should include designing recruitment posters as part of your marketing materials (see Chapter 10: Marketing and customer care) for distribution to training colleges. Once you have taken on good staff you will want to look after them.

INTERNAL CUSTOMERS

Staff should be seen as 'internal customers', which means that you should endeavour to meet their needs as comprehensively as possible (see Chapter 10: Marketing and customer care). Good induction, a comprehensive training programme, an effective appraisal system and clearly defining their role will all contribute.

In general, try to use any experience that staff may bring to the team and which is additional to their childcare skills. For example, if one member of your staff is keen on sport, you may wish to encourage him/her to take greater responsibility for the children's physical exercise routines. If another speaks a foreign language, s/he could spend a little time every day with the older groups introducing a few words and ideas from another culture. This approach benefits the nursery and adds interest to the role for the member of staff involved.

With regard to salary levels, pay as much as you know you can afford. The status and pay levels of early years professionals are still inadequate for the valuable role they perform but you will also have to be realistic about what salary costs you can sustain. Remember that retention of good staff is vital to continuity of care for the children.

APPRAISALS

As part of your system of management, you would be advised to include appraisals. Research shows that staff perform better if they understand what is expected of them, how their performance will be assessed and how well they are doing. Carried out successfully, appraisals will encourage job satisfaction, achievement and commitment.

An effective appraisal system aims to encourage constant monitoring of work and provide feedback on performance. A good system will deliver the following objectives:

- *provide constant review of past performance and objectives*

- *give praise and recognition for achievements at work*

- *set new goals and objectives in line with the nursery's plans*

- *identify any training needs*

- *improve motivation and communication*

In the short term, appraisals present an addition to the workload but the nursery will benefit from the long-term benefits of a better-motivated team.

12: CASE STUDIES

SOUND BUSINESS SKILLS, thorough preparation, hard work and utter determination have combined to produce some highly successful nurseries and nursery chains in recent years.

SCAMPS, MACCLESFIELD

In 1988 when Maureen Collins and Kate Barnes needed childcare, the nearest day nursery to their home town of Macclesfield in Cheshire was half an hour away. They decided to go into partnership and set up their own.

Neither of them had a childcare background – Maureen had been a dental hygienist and Kate had run her own small business in computer training. They contacted the nursery registration officer at their local authority who was 'extremely helpful'. She visited them at Maureen's home and explained what was required to set up a nursery and gave them a copy of the local guidelines.

Maureen and Kate began looking for premises and found an old, pre-fabricated ex-council nursery for rent on council-owned land. The premises had not been used as a nursery for a year and was in need of renovation. Between them they drew up a business plan and took it to Midland Bank. They built up a good understanding with the local manager and after detailed discussion, he agreed to lend them £10,000. Kate says, 'We had no capital to put in ourselves and the bank manager was really helpful. We built up a great relationship with him. I think it's very important to find someone you can work well with.'

Recognising that they needed qualified childcare skills on their team, they recruited an experienced nursery officer. Together they began the process of advertising and through the local paper they recruited the rest of the team. Many of the staff they initially recruited, including their deputy, are still with them.

They negotiated a lease with the council, which included the first year rent free, and used the £10,000 to renovate the nursery. By chance, they were able to buy equipment second hand from a local playgroup which was closing down. Being the first full-day nursery to open in Macclesfield, they received considerable publicity in the local press. They put up notices in post offices and local playgroups and advertised an open day at the nursery.

Disaster struck when, the night before the open day, a workman prodded a water tank in the roof to show Maureen that it would need replacing at 'some time' and the tank emptied its contents all over the newly decorated bathrooms in the nursery. They had to spend the night cleaning and redecorating.

The open day was a huge success and they took deposits covering the first month's fees from several parents. By the end of three months the 30-place nursery was operating at 85 per cent occupancy and they had avoided any early trading losses.

They spent the next year working up to 15 hours a day cooking, cleaning and handling the administration, paying themselves 'peanuts'. They rapidly developed an excellent reputation in the community and after only a year's trading added a further 20 places to the premises, which filled quickly.

After three years' trading the recession began to affect their profits and they were forced to make some changes to compensate. They wrote a second business plan, adjusted the level of fees and agreed with parents that they paid by standing order. An optional short day was introduced, which helped retain business and an overdraft was agreed with the bank.

They had always known that the pre-fabricated building would not last long and experience had given them a vision of how a nursery should be. So, as the recession faded, they began planning their dream nursery. The first thing they needed to do was to agree a long lease on the land so that they could recoup the capital spent on a new building. They began discussions with the borough council officers, who in turn had to seek the charity commissioners' permission to lease the land to Scamps as the land was held on trust. It was 12 months before they responded.

During this time Maureen and Kate had designed the new nursery themselves and had a surveyor translate the plans into working drawings. They had arranged insurance, negotiated with the builder, agreed a commercial mortgage with the bank and an additional business loan from the local Training Enterprise Council.

Eighteen months later the builder was on site ready to start work and Maureen and Kate were waiting only for council permission to proceed. Their solicitor called to inform the council that the £3,000 cheque covering the council's fees for the lease agreement was being hand delivered. The council replied that they would have to delay five days until the cheque cleared. In response, Kate and Maureen went straight to the bank with a small rucksack and took out £3,000 in £5 notes. They marched into the council offices and, having made their point, were given the necessary agreement that day. In April 1999 Kate and Maureen's new, 71-place purpose-built nursery opened.

The nursery is profitable and is nearly full most days. Their reputation locally is still excellent and they have just received their latest Ofsted inspection, which was very positive. They know a number of families whose children first attended the nursery 11 years ago and whose siblings are there today.

Kate puts their success down to the quality of the staff team, many of whom have been with them for more than five years, and the benefits of her partnership with Maureen. 'We bring different skills to the nursery and it works well,' she says. It has been very much Kate and Maureen's business and together they have built a close working relationship. They both admit that if they had the choice, they would do it all again.

CHILD & CO, OXFORDSHIRE

In 1990, Lesley Millar was coming to the end of her MBA course while working as a corporate design manager. Her husband was in the RAF working in the Ministry of Defence in London. Lesley was looking for her next career move and thought that the day-nursery sector would be ideal to bring together her business skills and earlier experience as a reception class teacher. So, she began a holiday playscheme in a local primary school near her home in Wallingford.

Lesley enjoyed working with the children and saw a need for childcare so she approached the local bank manager for a small overdraft. She had to provide a detailed business plan laid out to the bank's specification before they agreed to the overdraft.

During this time Lesley had continued to network with her MBA colleagues and it was through this route that she discovered that Mount Vernon Hospital in Northwood was considering nursery care for their staff's children. She met with the facilities department and after several meetings she involved another local employer, BP Engineering. After considerable planning, the hospital agreed to provide suitable leased accommodation, BP provided the equipment and in early 1991 the first Child & Co nursery opened on a management contract.

Lesley had taken considerable care over staff recruitment, and under her management the nursery quickly developed a good reputation. Northwick Park NHS Trust in Harrow saw the benefits that the Mount Vernon nursery had provided for their staff and asked to meet her to discuss a facility in their grounds. She met with the Trust and involved Midland Bank, which had identified a need for childcare in the area. Between the three parties they provided a Portakabin and equipment and in late 1991 Lesley's second nursery opened at Northwick Park, providing 43 places to the children of hospital employees.

The following year AEA Technology tendered for the operation of their newly built nursery in Winfrith, near Dorchester. Lesley thought that the tender offered a good opportunity to expand the company and responded. Against more experienced competition she was awarded the contract and took on the staff to manage the nursery. A team from Bournemouth University, which had been considering providing childcare for staff and students, then visited the Winfrith nursery and invited Child & Co to help set up a facility on its Talbot campus. The university provided a 30-place purpose-built unit and Lesley and her team took over the operation in early 1994. At the same time the company set up a small nursery in leased premises in a former school in Mongewell Park near Wallingford, Oxfordshire.

A year later, not far from Wallingford, a former village school came up for rent and Child & Co took a long lease from the Church of England. The extensive refurbishments were paid for from the company's trading profits and a 60-place nursery in the picturesque village of Great Haseley opened in 1995.

In late 1995, a Victorian house became available in Earley, Reading and with another business plan, Lesley gained approval from the bank for a commercial mortgage of 75 per cent of the purchase value. Over £200,000 for the balance of the purchase, the refurbishment and equipment came from company profits and the 63-place Abbeymore nursery was added to the portfolio.

Up to this point, Lesley had been running the company with a small, dedicated team from makeshift offices. In early 1994 the company was able to borrow the required funds from the bank to buy a large Victorian mansion set in four acres of grounds in Wallingford for conversion into a 63-place nursery, central office accommodation and a company training centre.

The Child & Co strategy was successful in keeping the company's borrowing low against the value of its assets. More importantly it enabled slow but steady growth, which meant that Lesley was always able to set, maintain and monitor the quality of care given by each nursery.

For the next two years the company traded profitably and continued to maintain an excellent reputation. Then the advent of Government-funded nursery vouchers for all four-year-olds brought Ofsted inspections to nurseries. Group 4 received a contract from Ofsted to co-ordinate the inspections programme. They selected a number of operators and entered into partnerships to conduct the inspections. Child & Co was considered ideal because of the quality of its own provision. At this point Lesley's husband had left the RAF and joined the company, and he took over the inspection side of the business.

Further expansion plans were realised through the company's contacts at Mount Vernon & Watford NHS Trust and suitable premises were found to replace a former nursery on the Watford hospital site. The bank agreed to assist with another commercial mortgage for 75 per cent of the value and the remainder along with costs of refurbishment were met from operating profits. The Park Nursery opened in January 1998 providing 63 places for children of staff at the hospital and for local residents. Meanwhile, the nursery at Mount Vernon had outgrown its original building and a 125-pace nursery was established on the site through an imaginative building project which linked two former nurses' homes.

July 1999 saw the opening of Child & Co's ninth nursery in leased premises in Abingdon. The new nursery, called St Mary's after an Anglican order which ran a school in the building many years before, provides 50 places for local children in a converted Victorian building set in considerable grounds. And in September 1999 the company took over the operation of Scott's House, an independent school in Witney, Oxfordshire. The school includes a day nursery and can take up to 115 children aged from three months to eight years.

In the ten years of its existence, Child & Co has grown from a summer playscheme to a nursery group operating 10 nurseries, handling hundreds of nursery inspections and employing over 150 staff. The company turnover is more than £3m. Child & Co has won a number of business awards and Lesley has been named Woman of the Year three times.

So to what does she attribute her success? Obviously sound business skills play their part, along with thorough preparation, hard work and utter determination. Lesley's own vision of a childcare company providing a standard of care which exceeds parents' expectations and her principle of always seeking the best for children has played a large part in the company's achievement. However, she has always acknowledged that underpinning the success of Child & Co is a dedicated, professional staff team sharing the same ideals for quality.

Whether working directly with the children, as ancillary staff or within the head office, she recognises that each employee has played a vital role in ensuring the quality of service which has become the Child & Co trademark. In return, Lesley has provided support, training and career opportunities. She has also ensured that communications, in-company and between the staff and parents, have been of the highest standard.

The company pays considerable attention to recruitment, acknowledging that it is important to seek the best staff from the outset. Lesley explains: 'We ask all applicants to fill in a comprehensive application form and then we invite those that are short-listed for interview and assessment. At the interview stage we often ask them to work alongside children to demonstrate their skills and for senior positions we expect them to give a presentation on some aspect of childcare.'

At Child & Co staff training is ongoing and the training and development manager holds regular seminars and workshops at the training centre in Wallingford. Specialists are brought in to deliver a programme tailored for key staff members. The company also operates several modern apprenticeships and traineeships in childcare and education. The result is that nearly 50 per cent of senior posts in the nurseries are filled through internal promotion – a sign of a company training its own future.

Remarkably, throughout the period of growth, the company has done little marketing. It has advertised occasionally and produces parent information about each nursery but customers have come from word of mouth. Its reputation for quality childcare has played a large role in the company's success.

THE BIRRELL COLLECTION, EDINBURGH

Yvonne Birrell entered the nursery business by the side door. Frustrated by the system, she left behind a good career in teaching and admits today that 'there have been very few days when I have regretted that decision.'

While working in primary school teaching, Yvonne realised that there were three important ingredients in making a good school: strong staff team spirit, a leader with a consultative style and a large enough budget to buy the appropriate resources. Yvonne felt that she could create all three ingredients and in 1988 set out to do so.

She planned to offer full-day care to three- to five-year-olds and spent much time searching for premises until it dawned on her that her spacious flat with a garden in the heart of Edinburgh's financial centre was ideal. This gave her the advantage of starting cheaply and as child numbers increased, her flatmates decreased. Nine months later every room in the flat was used for childcare and the nursery had required only £3,000 to open.

In 1990, after two years of persuasion from parents to provide nursery care in other parts of the city, she began to consider expanding. With virtually no capital, she set about planning to adapt the underused buildings in colleges, universities and hospitals. She identified that they could benefit from additional revenue from her rent and that she could benefit from well-resourced surroundings for the nurseries and additional customers from employees. Her next two nurseries opened in a college and a hospital.

All three sites had been rented and to develop some security, Yvonne decided to approach Abbey National for capital to buy a property for conversion into a nursery. Her business had shown steady growth over three years and the lender was impressed that she had taken very little out of the company during that time. In 1992, Abbey National provided a loan to buy a Victorian building on the fringe of Edinburgh's city centre which was converted into Yvonne's fourth nursery and some residential accommodation. This purchase drained resources which temporarily limited her expansion.

After years of planning, in September 1998, one of Yvonne's goals was realised when the first Birrell Collection purpose-built nursery opened in Edinburgh. Starting with a greenfield site and incorporating all the design features that she wanted was, says Yvonne 'a wonderful opportunity'. She acknowledges that the process, including weekly site meetings with builders, was a steep learning curve but the nursery filled quickly, being well-located, and staffed by an experienced team.

When asked to discuss any setbacks over the ten years, Yvonne replies, ' I don't recall any real disasters, but there has been the odd disappointment. The usual handful of failed planning applications and missed properties which can be a killer to morale and motivation.'

During the growth of the Birrell Collection Nursery Schools, Yvonne ventured into offering workplace childcare, but stopped after a three-year trial. She recalls the lessons learnt: 'Essentially, when considering working in partnership, it is vital to ensure before you start that your values, beliefs and objectives are in harmony with your potential partner.'

Yvonne is now focusing on strengthening the infrastructure of the company, developing staff through in-service training and increasing the capacity of two of the existing nurseries.

Yvonne recognises that the nursery business has changed since she started. More of her time is spent immersed in paperwork, however she still finds time to spend with the children. 'One day recently I was modelling for a group of children who were crafting facial features from dough,' she says. 'A two-year-old was labouring intently on rolling out two long, thin sausage shapes – squinting occasionally at my face for reference. Painstakingly, she positioned these just above my eyes on her drawing. Impressed by her observation skills, I exclaimed, "How clever Lauren, you've remembered my eyebrows." Puzzled, she replied, "These aren't your eyebrows, these are your wrinkles!"'

BIBLIOGRAPHY

R Bolles Richard *What Colour Is Your Parachute?* Ten Speed Press (1970)

The British Venture Capital Association Directory British Venture Capital Assocation (1998)

Childcare Works The Daycare Trust (1997)

M Dudek *Kindergarten Architecture* E&FN Spon (1996)

Greenhouse Consultancy market research

R Harrison, University of Ulster, Techinvest Seminar (January, 1999)

Independent Day Nursery Workforce Survey prepared by The Local Government Management Board (1998)

H Jameson and M Watson *Starting and Running a Nursery* Stanley Thornes (1998)

P Leach *Children First* Penguin (1994)

Social Trends 28 Office for National Statistics (1998)

Starting a Nursery, Nursery World (Summer 1999)

S Williams *Lloyds Bank Small Business Guide* Penguin Group (1987)

USEFUL CONTACTS

Advisory, Conciliation and
Arbitration Service (ACAS)
83 Euston Road
London NW1 2RB
Telephone: 0171 396 0022

A H Lansley (nursery agent)
111 Oxford Road
Reading
Berkshire RG1 7UH
Telephone: 0118 959 0271

British Chambers of Commerce
Manning House
22 Carlisle Place
London SW1P 1JA
Telephone: 0171 565 2000

The British Venture Capital
Association Directory
12 Essex Street
London
WC2 3AA
Telephone: 0171 240 3846
Internet: http://www.brainstorm.co.uk/BVCA

Business Link Signpost Line (for information
about local Business Link Offices)
Telephone: 0171 224 1600

CACI Ltd (market research company)
CACI House
Kensington Village
Avonmore Road
London W14 8TS
Telephone: 0171 602 6000

Chesterton plc (valuer)
54 Brook Street
London W1A 2BU
Telephone: 0171 499 0404

Christie & Co (valuer)
London Office telephone: 0171 227 0700
Branches throughout the UK

Companies Registration Office
Companies House
Crown Way
Maindy
Cardiff CF4 3UZ
Telephone: 01222 380801

Cottrell & Vermuelen Architecture
1a Iliffe Street
London SE17 3LJ
Telephone: 0171 708 2567

Council for Awards in Children's Education (CACHE)
8 Chequer Street
St Alban's
Herfordshire AL1 3XZ
Telephone: 01727 847 636

The Daycare Trust
4 Wild Court
London WC2B 4AU
Telephone: 0171 405 5617

Department for Education and Employment (DfEE)
Sanctuary Buildings
Great Smith Street
London SW1P 3BT
Telephone: 0171 925 5000

Experian Ltd (market research company)
Embankment House
Electric Avenue
Nottingham NG2 1RP
Telephone: 0115 941 0888

Global Mobile (modular/prefab buildings company)
The Gatehouse
Ruck Lane
Horsmonden
Kent TN12 8EA
Telephone: 01892 722733

Greenhouse Childcare Consultancy
The Old Post Office Cottage
Church Lane
Rainow
Cheshire SK10 5XE
Telephone: 01625 575594

Health and Safety Executive (HSE)
Information Centre
Broad Lane
Sheffield SH3 7HQ
Telephone: 0114 291 2300

Institute of Personnel and Development (IPD)
35 Camp Road
London SW19
Telephone: 0181 971 9000

Kiddicare (insurance broker)
Suffolk House
3 Sorrel Horse Mews
Ipswich
Suffolk IP4 1LN
Telephone: 01473 216406

Land Registry
32 Lincolns Inn Fields
London WC2A 3PH
Telephone: 0171 917 8888

Loan Guarantee Scheme
Department of Trade and Industry
St Mary's House
Moorfoot
Sheffield S1 4PQ
Telephone: 01142 597 308

National Day Nurseries Association (NDNA)
16 New North Parade
Huddersfield
West Yorkshire HD1 5JP
Telephone: 01484 541641

National Early Years Network
77 Holloway Road
London N7 8JZ
Telephone: 0171 607 9573

National School Transfer (nursery agent)
Tilshead House
Tilshead
Salisbury
Wilts SP3 4RX
Telephone: 01980 621251

Office for Standards in Education (Ofsted)
Alexandra House
Kingsway
London WC2
Telephone: 0171 421 6800

Pinders (valuer)
Pinder House
Central Milton Keynes
MK9 1DS
Telephone: 01908 350500

Portakabin Ltd (modular/prefab buildings company)
New Lane
Huntington
York YO32 9PT
Telephone: 01904 611655

Pre-School Learning Alliance
69 King's Cross Road
London WC1X 9LL
Telephone: 0171 833 0991

Prince's Youth Business Trust
18 Park Square East
London NW1 4LH
Telephone: 0171 543 1234

Qualifications and Curriculum Authority (QCA)
29 Bolton Street
London W1Y 7PD
Telephone: 0171 509 5555

School Transfer Consultants (STC)
(nursery agent)
Haydon Cross
Dale Road
Southfleet
Kent DA13 9NX
Telephone: 01474 534151

Scottish Independent Nurseries
Association (SINA)
9 Saughton Hall Gardens
Edinburgh EH12 5RD
Telephone: 0131 467 8676

The Small Firms Service
Department of Trade and Industry
1 Victoria Street
London SW1H OET
Telephone: 0171 215 5000

Speaks Building Systems Ltd
(modular/prefab buildings company)
Shay Lane Works
Shay Lane
Ovenden
Halifax HX3 6SF
Telephone: 01422 353022

Spencer Meakin & Newbroad Ltd
(insurance broker)
196 Tonge Moor Road
Tonge Moor
Bolton BL2 2HN
Telephone: 01204 525279

The Stationery Office (formerly HSMO)
Book shops located in London, Belfast,
Birmingham and Manchester
General enquiries telephone: 0171 873 0011

Sweet William Nursery Insurance
William Taylor House
Derry Avenue
South Ockendon
Essex RM15 5DL
Telephone: 01708 855141

Taylors *(valuer)*
Court House
Mill Court
Featherstone Road
Wolverton Mill
Milton Keynes MK12 5QS
Telephone: 01908 226611

Terrapin *(modular/prefab buildings company)*
Bond Avenue
Bletchley
Milton Keynes MK1 1JJ
Telephone: 01908 270900

Tingdene *(modular/prefab buildings company)*
Bradfield Road
Finedon Road Industrial Estate
Wellingborough
Northamptonshire NN8 4HB
Telephone: 01933 225157